I0795190

THE ARISTOCRAT AND THE ABLE SEAMAN

THE ARISTOCRAT AND THE ABLE SEAMAN

THE COUNTESS OF ROTHES, THOMAS JONES, AND THE TRAGEDY OF TITANIC

ANGELA YOUNG

The History Press

Dedicated to
Noël Rothes and Thomas Jones
with admiration and respect

First published 2026

The History Press
97 St George's Place, Cheltenham,
Gloucestershire, GL50 3QB
www.thehistorypress.co.uk

British Library Cataloguing in Publication Data.
A catalogue record for this book is available from the British Library.

ISBN 978 1 83705 114 4

Typesetting and origination by The History Press
Printed and bound in Great Britain by TJ Books, Padstow, Cornwall.

FSC www.fsc.org MIX Paper | Supporting responsible forestry FSC® C013056

The History Press proudly supports
Trees for Life
www.treesforlife.org.uk

EU Authorised Representative: Easy Access System Europe
Mustamäe tee 50, 10621 Tallinn, Estonia
gpst.request@easproject.com

Contents

Introduction

It's difficult to imagine a time when people didn't know much about *Titanic*, but it wasn't until forty-three years after the disaster when Walter Lord's book *A Night to Remember* was published in 1955 that interest revived. In the aftermath of the sinking, in 1912, when the press uproar died down and the Inquiries concluded, *Titanic*'s survivors rarely talked about what happened. They were in shock, they had what we'd call PTSD and, in 1914, just two years after *Titanic* sank, war broke out. The terrible number of deaths when the world's largest liner sank – 1,496 people died[1] – was eclipsed by the millions who died in the First World War.

In the introduction to the fiftieth-anniversary edition of Lord's book, published in 2005, the American historian Nathaniel Philbrick wrote that *A Night to Remember* was the 'first significant book about *Titanic* for nearly forty years'.[2] The book was made from interviews with sixty-three survivors, including a written interview with my great-grandmother, Lucy Noël Martha Leslie, Countess of Rothes, the Aristocrat of this book. (Rothes is pronounced *Roth*-iz: roth rhymes with moth. Rothes is the title; Leslie is the family name.)

My own family's interest in *Titanic* revived when Noël Rothes died in 1956 and her eldest son, Malcolm, and his eldest daughter, Jean Mackenzie, found a box of Noël's *Titanic* papers – papers they'd

A Night to Remember by Walter Lord, first published in 1955, from interviews with sixty-three *Titanic* survivors. The book and the film revived interest in *Titanic* over forty years after the disaster. This is the 1976 illustrated edition cover. (Image © Ken Carroll, designer. Reproduced with his permission)

never seen. There were newspaper cuttings from 1912 and a copy of Noël's sworn statement to the British Vice-Consul at Altadena, California, made that May, a month after the disaster. There were letters from the Able Seaman of this book, Thomas William Jones, and some of Noël's own letters; there were letters from Maria-Josefa de Satode Peñasco y Castellana (birth name Perez de Soto y Vallejo) who survived in Lifeboat Number 8, the lifeboat that Thomas Jones commanded and Noël Rothes helped to steer. There were straightforward accounts of the disaster and emotional outpourings. I've quoted from Noël's papers throughout this book and I've included photographs of Jones' original letters.

Noël's *Titanic* papers counteract the myths that made her remark occasionally afterwards, 'Do remember that whatever you hear about the *Titanic* is not true.'[3]

Thomas Jones' youngest daughter, Nell Jones, wrote that when the film of *A Night to Remember* was released in July 1958, the press pestered her father and he became ill. He didn't want to talk to them; he didn't want to remember. As Dr Rudi Newman, the travel historian and author, writes, *A Night to Remember* is still the most historically accurate film, because of its thorough research and, 'Because several survivors assisted with its production',[4] so it must have been particularly difficult for *Titanic*'s survivors to watch. Jones' granddaughter, Shelagh Oakes, who was only 14 at the time, remembered her mother, Mary Ada Oakes, Jones' eldest daughter, saying her father was very upset by the film's publicity. Jones' *Titanic* memories clearly still held the power to traumatise him forty-six years later. Mary Ada said he was 'never the same', even after the publicity died down: it brought back memories he couldn't bear to repeat to the press when they 'badgered' him.

In his book, *Shadow of the Titanic*, the journalist and writer Andrew Wilson wrote:

> This forced forgetting – the conscious or unconscious suppression of memory – was one of the many strategies employed by those who survived. For them, the experience was like a

> closed book, a text that had been placed in a strongbox and locked away from both prying strangers and curious family members. It was a subject not open for analysis or discussion.[5]

The box that Noël's son and granddaughter found when she died was her strongbox: it held the things she didn't want to remember, things her family hadn't known.

In 1980, twenty-four years after Noël Rothes died, Eve Mackworth-Young, my mother, Malcolm's second daughter, typed Noël's handwritten material (which hasn't been published before) and put it, and all the newspaper cuttings and other material, into several albums. Many years afterwards I developed a talk about the 'Aristocrat and the Able Seaman' from the material in my mother's albums and quite often, after the talk, people ask if there's a book. This is that book.

I discovered more about Twm (Tom) Titanic – as they call him where he was born, in Cemaes Bay in north Anglesey, Wales – from Shelagh Oakes and from Eric Torr, the Chairman of the Cemaes Bay History Group (pronounced Kemus). Carys Davies, Elfed Jones (no relation) of Oriel Cemaes and J. Richard Williams, who live and work in Cemaes Bay, also told me about him and I read a biography at *Encyclopedia Titanica*.[6] In 2012, the centenary of the sinking, I met Nell Jones when the BBC interviewed us about our ancestors.[7]

As I researched and discovered what Noël Rothes and Thomas Jones went through on that terrifying night, I realised it was possible that many more who sailed on *Titanic* might have survived. Through the papers of these two courageous survivors, through evidence to the Inquiries from the *Titanic Inquiry Project*, where complete texts of the American and British Inquiries can be read[8] and from which the *Titanic* researcher Robert Ottmers has kindly given me permission to quote, and through my own research, I've clearly seen the mistakes and miscalculations that cost the lives of 1,496 people. These things have been examined and documented by *Titanic* experts for a long time now but – as I frequently discover after my talk – they often fail to reach ordinary folk like me.

Noël thought there were enough lifeboats for everyone, so why weren't there? Jones thought he was rowing his lifeboat towards the lights of a rescue ship, so why weren't they rescued? Both heard the screams and cries of those dying in the icy waters behind them but they, and *Titanic*'s owners, thought the great ship 'practically unsinkable' and a 'lifeboat in itself',[9] so why wasn't it?

I've consulted *Titanic* experts to make sure that what you're about to read is as accurate and myth-free as possible (any remaining errors are my own) and my intention – despite Noël's and Jones' silence afterwards – is to tell their *Titanic* stories, in some aspects for the first time, precisely because they couldn't bear to. I want to show how their courage, kindness, resourcefulness, thoughtfulness, steadfastness and seafaring knowledge on that terrible night helped twenty-five others, and how the things they witnessed prompted my exploration of what happened (without the exaggerations) so that I can make the facts better known to people like me who aren't *Titanic* experts: to give us a clearer understanding of what went wrong, why so few survived and how Maritime Law changed afterwards to make life at sea safer.

But above all, *The Aristocrat and the Able Seaman* is my tribute to two courageous people who – like everyone else on board the White Star Line's magnificent new liner – never dreamt that the great ship would sink.

One

In the Beginning

Anticipating the future very keenly[1]

Lucy Noël Martha Leslie, Countess of Rothes, and Thomas William Jones would never have met but for the disaster. The only thing they had in common on the day they boarded *Titanic* at Southampton, on Wednesday, 10 April 1912, was their age: she was born on 25 December 1878 (and so was always known by her second name, Noël); he was born on 15 November 1877. She was 33 and he was 34. But the stratification of British Edwardian society – mirrored by the differences between *Titanic*'s first-class decks and the crew-quarter decks – kept them apart until the collision (or allision as a vessel striking a stationary object is properly called, but I'll use collision). They'd have thought you extremely odd if you'd suggested they had anything in common at all but, despite their differences, the aristocrat and the able seaman worked fearlessly and harmoniously together in Lifeboat Number 8 on the night *Titanic* sank, doing everything they could for the sake of twenty-five others.

For years, accounts of the numbers of passengers and crew who sailed out into the north Atlantic from *Titanic*'s last landfall, Queenstown (Cobh, since 1921) in the south-west of Ireland and accounts of those who survived and those who died have varied.

Lucy Noël Martha Leslie, Countess of Rothes, *c.*1900. Passenger in Lifeboat Number 8. Always known, informally, by her second name, Noël, because she was born on Christmas day, 1878. (Unknown photographer. Image courtesy of the Leslie family)

Thomas William Jones, *c.*1900. The able seaman who commanded Lifeboat Number 8. Born on 15 November 1877. (Unknown photographer. Image courtesy of Shelagh Oakes)

Misspellings, omissions and aliases made accounting for them all an inexact science.[2] But, since 2011, all passenger and crew names have finally been accounted for and tallied correctly: 1,496 people died; 712 survived.[3]

Passengers and Crew								
	Men		Women		Children		Total	
Total Number of Passengers and Crew	1,663		442		103		2,208	
	Lost	Saved	Lost	Saved	Lost	Saved	Lost	Saved
Number Lost/ Saved	1,340	323	109	333	47	56	1,496	712

The numbers of passengers and crew who died and survived, from *Report into the Loss of the SS Titanic*, page 68, by George Behe, Samuel Halpern et al. (Image courtesy of Samuel Halpern)

But, to begin at the beginning, if you'd been standing on the White Star Dock at Southampton on Wednesday, 10 April 1912, you'd have seen people from all walks of life boarding the world's largest liner. First-class passengers carried their pets, while their precious possessions, including one car, were stowed. Third-class passengers carried smaller bags packed with everything they possessed. And if you'd been there in the days before the passengers boarded, you'd have seen crates of beer and wine, sacks of mail, food in unimaginable quantities and drinking water hoisted on board.

On that Wednesday in 1912, the ship's crew and their commander, Captain Edward Smith, busied themselves with last-minute checks, an inspection for the Board of Trade under immigration officer Maurice Clarke and the lowering of two rear starboard lifeboats – the only safety drill carried out on board *Titanic* after she left Belfast – while rich industrialists and bankers, politicians and people from the military, socialites and the titled were shown to their first-class cabins. Professors and writers, teachers, clergymen and tourists were shown to their second-class cabins, and migrants, people travelling from Armenia, Croatia, Russia and China; from Syria, Romania and Lebanon; from

Holland, Italy, Sweden and other European countries – people filled with dreams of better lives in America – were shown to their third-class cabins. For many migrants it was the first holiday of their lives and they were delighted to find their accommodation exactly as it had been advertised: of far better quality than second-class cabins on any other liner at the time.

Titanic's world was a very white one: there was only one Black person on board, Joseph Philippe Lemercier Laroche, a Haitian engineer. He travelled second class among the professionals with his white French wife, Juliette, and their two mixed-heritage daughters. He died in the disaster, but in 1912 his story was overlooked.[4] There were about 130 Greater Syrian passengers[5] (modern Syria, Lebanon, Jordan and Palestine) and eight Chinese[6] in third class; about thirty of the Greater Syrians and six Chinese survived. Between 1999 and 2001 the *Titanic* scholar Lester J. Mitcham compiled tables of passengers and crew that show 311 non-British subjects, or trans-migrant passengers (as they were called in 1912), only sixty-six of whom survived.[7]

One of Noël's press cuttings, from *The New York Herald*, Paris edition, dated 11 April 1912, the day after *Titanic* set sail from Southampton, reported on the embarking passengers. Under the title 'Leaves London for Farm' is written:

> The Countess of Rothes, who is also a passenger, said she was going out to join her husband who had bought some fruit land in the West. 'We will return to England in July,' she added, 'and then take our children over to the United States.' Asked how she liked the idea of leaving London society for a Californian fruit farm, Lady Rothes said she was anticipating the future very keenly.[8]

In the New York edition of the same newspaper, Noël was quoted as being 'full of joyful expectation'. So many people who set out on board *Titanic*, particularly the migrants, were full of joyful expectation, but so few survived.

In the Marconi Room the ship's two young Radio Operators, Jack Phillips and Harold Bride, were already sending passengers' Marconigrams. This brand-new technology meant people could tell their friends far more quickly than by letter exactly how the great ship lived up to their expectations: the luxurious fittings and the interior designs were as good if not better than the best hotels in the world. But the Radio Operators were also keen to use the Marconi technology for its secondary but still important purpose: communicating with other ships about changes in the weather; about their course and any alterations their Captain might make; about any obstructions to their passage. Important messages about navigation were given the prefix MSG (for Master Service Gram): these messages had to be acknowledged by the Captain, but if the MSG prefix was forgotten the message might not be given to him.

If you'd been standing on the White Star Dock that Wednesday in April 1912, you'd have heard the ship's whistles pierce the air at noon to tell anyone who wasn't sailing to disembark, and you'd have seen her mooring lines released. You'd have watched the passengers lifting their hats and waving their handkerchiefs from the different decks as *Titanic* steamed from Southampton: passengers who'd been transferred from other ships that were unable to leave Southampton because of the miners' strike; passengers who'd chosen this ship because it was her maiden voyage; because she was the largest liner in the world; because her accommodation outdid that of every other liner at the time. But most of all because of her safety and seaworthiness: because she was 'practically unsinkable' and 'a lifeboat in itself'.[9]

Titanic's great length exceeded the height of all but one of the greatest buildings and memorials on earth at the time. The largest building in the illustration on page 18, the New Woolworth Building in New York (to the left of the ship), was, until 1929, the tallest building in the world at 792ft. *Titanic*'s length was 882.6ft, 96ft 6in longer, but she was shorter than the Eiffel Tower by 200ft. It's interesting, isn't it, that the White Star Line chose *not* to include the French monument in their publicity, but *Titanic was* the largest *moving* object in the world and while she was being built, at the great Harland & Wolff shipyard in Belfast, an observer described her as:

> A ship so monstrous and unthinkable that it towered over the buildings and dwarfed the very mountains by the water.[10]

Juliette Laroche wrote about *Titanic*'s size as she and her family travelled towards her from Cherbourg harbour: 'If you could see this monster: our tender looked like a fly compared to her.'[11] But if you superimpose *Titanic* on an image of a contemporary liner she looks surprisingly small.[12]

Noël Rothes sailed with her parents, Thomas and Clementina Dyer-Edwardes; Gladys Cherry, her husband's cousin; and her ladies' maid, Roberta Maioni. She was sailing to meet her husband, Norman Evelyn Leslie, the 19th Earl of Rothes, in New York.

It's interesting that the White Star Line chose not to include the Eiffel Tower in this publicity image. At 1,083ft (330m) it 'surpasses' *Titanic*'s 882.6ft (269m) by 200ft (61m). (Image courtesy of Dr Rudi Newman PhD, Transport Historian and Author)

She left behind two young sons at Leslie House, the family seat in Fife, Scotland: Malcolm, aged 10, and John (Jock), aged 2. By the time she boarded *Titanic*, Noël had been running Leslie House for almost ten years. By the time Thomas Jones boarded *Titanic* he'd been working for the White Star Line for just over ten years. The differences between these two people were stark.

An able seaman must be able, at a moment's notice, to paint, repair and clean a ship; to overhaul and operate the lifeboats, which became crucial in Jones' case; to stand watch and look out for obstructions in the way of a liner; and to take part in safety drills. He wasn't on lookout duty on the fatal night. In his evidence to the American Inquiry into the disaster, given on 25 April 1912,[13] Jones gave his address as 68 Nesfield Street, Liverpool, England. He was born to a family of seafarers: his parents were Griffith and Mary Jones (birth name Williams); his father was a sea Captain. When *Titanic* left Southampton, Thomas Jones was still a single man, although he'd met his future wife, Clara Moulton.

Among the other passengers was a science teacher, Lawrence Beesley, travelling second class. Unlikely as it may seem, he had his photograph taken while sitting on an exercise bicycle in the ship's gymnasium before *Titanic* left Southampton. He was an important witness to the disaster: he wrote about it in his book, *The Loss of the Titanic*, published just two months after the sinking, in June 1912. He might have said, because he was a science teacher, that all human beings have at least some things in common, but Noël, Jones and Beesley would have thought you very odd if you'd suggested that two of them would meet in a much smaller boat in just over four days' time, or that the third would find himself in another of those small boats, and all three – and 2,205 others – would witness an unthinkable, unimaginable disaster.

But on that Wednesday in April 1912, none of this troubled *Titanic*'s passengers as they found their cabins and the dining rooms; as the first- and second-class passengers marvelled at the swimming pool, the Turkish baths, the squash and racquets court and the gymnasium; as they found the reading and writing room, the smoking room and the library and walked along the promenade decks to wave goodbye to those below on the dock; as the third-class passengers settled into their unusually luxurious accommodation or joined others on deck to wave goodbye; as the rich and the poor, the titled and the migrants, the monied and the professionals all looked forward with innocent expectation to their safe arrival in New York.

Before *Titanic* steamed out into the Solent she narrowly avoided a collision with a much smaller steamer, the *New York*, in Southampton Water. *The New York Herald* article that described Noël leaving London for a Californian fruit farm began with this account:

> LONDON, Thursday [11 April 1912] – The departure yesterday from Southampton of the huge White Star Liner *Titanic*, the largest ship in the world, on her maiden voyage to New York, was almost marred by a disaster similar to that which befell the *Olympic* last September [*Olympic*, *Titanic*'s sister ship, captained by Edward Smith, collided with the Royal Navy ship the *Hawke* on 20 September 1911]. While the *Titanic* was being towed down Southampton Water by three tugs, the liner *New York*, moored alongside the quay, broke her cables .... When she came opposite the *New York* the seven hawsers holding the *New York* to the quay began to strain.
>
> That she was being drawn towards the passing liner by suction could not be doubted. Suddenly there was a noise like minute guns going off .... The seven hawsers holding the *New York* to the quay had broken. Immediately the stern of the vessel began to veer round towards the *Titanic*.
>
> Hasty megaphone orders were given aboard the liner and many of the passengers appeared to be in a state of great excitement. Presently the *Titanic* came to a standstill, and as soon as the hawsers had been disconnected the three tugs went to the assistance of the *New York*. At this time barely fifteen feet separated the two vessels. Fortunately the tugs were able to secure the *New York* and get her back to the quay without mishap.[14]

It is a dark irony that *Titanic* very nearly collided with a ship called the *New York*, a city she would never reach.

At the first landfall of the voyage, Cherbourg, Noël waved goodbye to her parents as the tender took them ashore: they were on their way to their château in Normandy. Later, Noël would be overwhelmingly grateful that her father hadn't sailed across the north Atlantic with her because, after *Titanic* collided with the iceberg, the men were asked to stand back so the women and children could board the lifeboats first. And because there weren't enough lifeboats, he almost certainly would have died.

Afterwards Noël wrote a long letter to her parents from the rescue ship the *Carpathia*. In it she said, 'I am one of the lucky ones'. She said it for the obvious reason that she survived but also because she hadn't sailed out into the north Atlantic with any of her menfolk. Ida Straus, a first-class passenger who stood by Lifeboat Number 8 but never boarded it, chose to stay with her husband and die beside him. Others, convinced of *Titanic*'s unsinkability, chose to stay on board the warm, safe (as they thought) ship, rather than be lowered 75ft down *Titanic*'s mighty hull to the freezing sea in a tiny lifeboat in the dark.[15]

One of Noël's press cuttings quotes Mrs A.A. Dick, who was rescued with her husband in Lifeboat Number 3. She told *The New York Herald*, for the edition printed on 21 April 1912:

> We were indifferent about leaving the steamship, as we did not believe it was going to sink .... There was no evidence of panic while we were on board and I first laughed at the idea of the *Titanic* sinking.

For so very many of the men among *Titanic*'s passengers and crew there was no choice about whether or not to board a lifeboat. But as they left Cherbourg they had no idea of what was to come, just as those on shore who witnessed *Titanic*'s majestic passage away from Cherbourg towards Queenstown had no idea that this was the last they'd ever see of the world's largest liner.

Period postcard of *Titanic* leaving Southampton, 1912. (Image courtesy of Dr Rudi Newman)

Two

Inventions and Invincibility

You thought the ship was unsinkable, did you?[1]

Titanic's keel was laid at Harland & Wolff's shipyard in Belfast on 22 March 1909.[2] It took thousands of men two years and two months to build her; it took another ten months to fit her out. In the year *Titanic*'s keel was laid, newer, faster, more efficient turbine rotor engines were being tried, tested and perfected. But the White Star Line management was cautious about these new engines. They decided to install only one turbine rotor engine to drive her central propeller; they used the old-fashioned tried-and-tested steam reciprocating engines to drive her port and starboard propellers. That system was also more economical.[3]

And that's why if anyone expected Captain Edward Smith to attempt a transatlantic speed record across the north Atlantic they'd have been disappointed; he didn't have the horsepower. But he did have J. Bruce Ismay, the White Star Line's Chairman, on board and he might have tried to persuade his Captain to make the best possible speed to show off his fine new liner. Captain Smith himself was hoping to beat the maiden voyage north Atlantic crossing time of *Titanic*'s sister ship, the *Olympic*: she made a swift 21.43 knots.[4]

But in his evidence to the American Inquiry, Ismay said *Titanic* 'had never been at full speed'.[5] And it's true that *Titanic* never reached her top speed using all twenty-nine boilers, but she was travelling as fast as her twenty-four main boilers were capable of carrying her:[6] leading fireman Frederick Barrett testified that the white 'full speed' indicator light was showing in the boiler rooms at the time of the collision.[7]

In Senator William Alden Smith's concluding address to the US Senate Inquiry into the disaster on Tuesday, 28 May 1912, he said:

> In the face of … [ice] warnings, each revolution of her engines marked at the moment of the collision her highest speed of 24½ miles per hour [between 21 and 22 knots[8]].

He also said:

> I think the presence of Mr. Ismay and Mr. Andrews [one of *Titanic*'s designers] stimulated the ship to greater speed than it would have made under ordinary conditions, although I cannot fairly ascribe to either of them any instructions to this effect.[9]

Captain Rostron, of the *Carpathia*, said that if he'd been warned of icebergs *and* it was a clear night *and* he was sure of his position he would remain at full speed – it was standard practice, to clear the danger area as quickly as possible – although not if he'd been warned of an ice *field*.[10] And he agreed with Senator Smith when he asked if Captain Smith's course was 'appropriate, safe and wise'.[11]

Lawrence Beesley wrote that at least three ice warnings from other ships on the same route reached the Marconi Operators on *Titanic*'s last day at sea (there were actually seven[12]) and these warnings should have persuaded Captain Smith to slow down. Senator Smith said that Captain Smith's:

> Indifference to danger was one of the direct and contributing causes of this unnecessary tragedy … [as well as his]

> overconfidence [in his ship] and neglect to heed the oft-repeated warnings of his friends [about ice].[13]

Gladys Cherry wondered, in a letter to her mother written on board the *Carpathia*, why, when they were among ice, they 'did not slow down at all and were going 22 knots per hour'.[14] Lawrence Beesley suggested that the unconscious demand of transatlantic passengers:

> For speed ... may have tempted captains to take a risk they might otherwise not have done. [Passenger demands] gradually forced the pace to what it is at present .... All of us who have cried for greater speed must take our share in the responsibility.[15]

Bruce Ismay said, 'If a man can see far enough to clear ice, he is perfectly justified in going full speed.'[16] But for speed guaranteed at sea

A turbine rotor engine *c.*1909. Note the size of the men compared with the size of the engine. (Image courtesy of Michael Pocock and Maritime Quest)

in 1912, the Cunarders outdid the White Star Liners: if you think of them in terms of twentieth-century aircraft, the Cunarders were the Concordes of their time, the White Star Liners the Jumbo jets. The White Star Line's USP, as we'd say today, was luxury and comfort, not speed. The Cunarders were fitted with the new turbine rotor engines just as soon as they were tried and tested and they won the majority of Blue Ribands for speed in those days. The White Star Liners did win some Blue Ribands, but the Cunarders won almost three times their number (fourteen to five).[17]

Captain Rostron said that Captain Smith was 'on his proper track, where he ought to have been ... at this time of year'.[18] And among Noël Rothes' press cuttings was one from *The New York Herald*, dated 22 April 1912, in which Captain Knapp, a navy hydrographer, confirmed *Titanic* was following the southern, not the northern, route. He said she was on:

> The proper westbound course, and her position when the collision occurred was exactly on the course prescribed.

But, according to the Royal Meteorological Society:

> Near-freezing air from northeast Canada ... south of Newfoundland, assisted by the prevailing southward flow of the ocean's Labrador Current meant icebergs and sea ice were further south than usual for the time of year.[19]

When Thomas Scanlan, Counsel on behalf of the National Sailors' and Firemen's Union, asked Bruce Ismay if the steamship companies had agreed a more southern route across the Atlantic *after Titanic* sank, Ismay agreed that they had,[20] suggesting that an even more southerly route should have been taken by *Titanic*.

Noël Rothes travelled in a first-class White Star Line cabin (in her interview with *The New York Herald*, Paris edition, she called it her 'stateroom').[21] In her sworn statement she said her cabin was Number 77, on C Deck, shared with Gladys Cherry. Her grandson,

Ian Leslie, 21st Earl of Rothes, confirmed this, although in the interview Noël said their cabin was Number 77 on B Deck, but I think that's a misprint. In Gareth Russell's *The Ship of Dreams* her cabin number is given as C-77 – which corroborates her sworn statement and what her grandson said. Russell, the historian, writer and broadcaster, writes that Purser McElroy moved 'with breakneck speed' to reassign her cabin from C-37, which was too small. Roberta Maioni, Noël's ladies' maid, was assigned a first-class cabin two decks below, on E Deck.[22]

For the privilege of travelling first class, Noël paid £70 for the cabin she shared with Gladys Cherry.[23] At the time of writing, in terms of relative purchasing power, that's £9,350, which I think is a great deal of money to pay for what would have been a six-day voyage, however luxurious the accommodation. But Noël was the only child of a wealthy businessman – she could afford it. There were others in first class who paid significantly more than her. She also paid £15 10*s* for Roberta Maioni's first-class cabin on E Deck (£2,070 in 2025) and another £1 for train fares from London to Southampton, for a total of £86 10*s* (£11,560 in 2025).[24]

Second-class passengers, Lawrence Beesley among them, paid varying amounts, but far less than first-class passengers. Beesley paid £13 for his six-day voyage, or roughly £1,740 in 2025, while third-class passengers – the majority of whom were migrants – paid between £3 and £9, or between £400 and £1,200 in 2025, depending on the number of people in each cabin.[25] These prices were more expensive than third-class tickets on other smaller and less-comfortable ships, but one of the many unique things about *Titanic* was that her third-class, or steerage quarters – so-called because they were often near the ship's rudder and the vibrations were greater – were far better than on any other liner at the time.[26] There were unusually good washing facilities, which included showers, and there was a dining room – something very few travelling third-class could expect on other liners at the time, where they would be expected to eat at trestle tables set up outside their cabins and serve themselves 'cafeteria-style' from a small pantry.

'Until the early 1890s they even had to provide their own eating utensils.'[27] Not so on board *Titanic*.

The crew quarters were much more basic but Able Seaman Thomas Jones obviously wasn't paying for his quarters; he was working and being paid. His Account of Wages issued by the British Board of Trade for six days' work on board *Titanic* shows that he was paid £1 (or 3*s* 4*d* a day). £1, in relative income terms in 2025 would be £750. So Jones' annual salary, in 1912, if he worked for fifty weeks, or 351 days, would have been £58 10*s* (or £44,000 in 2025). The amount Noël paid for her stateroom, £9,350 in 2025, was not far off a *quarter* of Jones' total annual salary: another illustration of the vast social and economic differences between these two people.

Jones' Account of Wages also shows that although the White Star Line stopped all crew pay on 15 April 1912, the day *Titanic* sank, they did pay bonuses, possibly for compassionate reasons.[28] Jones' bonus amounted to twenty-six days' pay, or £4 6*s* 8*d* (£3,050 in 2025), so the total amount he was paid was £5 6*s* 8*d* (£3,800 in 2025). But obviously he'd only have been paid £1 if *Titanic* had arrived safely in New York, so the comparison of his £1 wage with Noël's £70 for her first-class stateroom holds. However … if you add the cost of Noël's ladies' maid's cabin (£15 10*s*) to what she paid for her own cabin, the total amounts to £85 10*s* (£11,420 in 2025).[29]

Titanic was built and fitted out towards the end of the Belle Époque (1871–1914). It was a time of peace in many parts of the world, a time of stability and prosperity, of optimism and, for many people, there was a sense of invincibility, a sense that you could do or be whatever you dreamt of doing or being. It was a time when people had *absolute faith* in science and technology.[30] Claes-Göran Wetterholm, *Titanic* historian, ethnologist and writer, said the engineer became society's high priest as churches began to lose their grip on human souls: there was a growing belief that *everything* was possible.[31] In such an atmosphere, imaginations flourished and inventions multiplied.

The first telephones and the first gramophones were made; the painters Sargent and Whistler were established or establishing

Olympic's Cabin B-69. Noël Rothes' *Titanic* cabin, C-77, was in the same style but it had portholes, not windows. Noël paid £70 for her cabin (£9,350 in 2025), almost a *quarter* of Jones' annual salary. (Image courtesy of Daniel Klistorner's Collection. Words adapted from Gareth Russell's *The Ship of Dreams*)

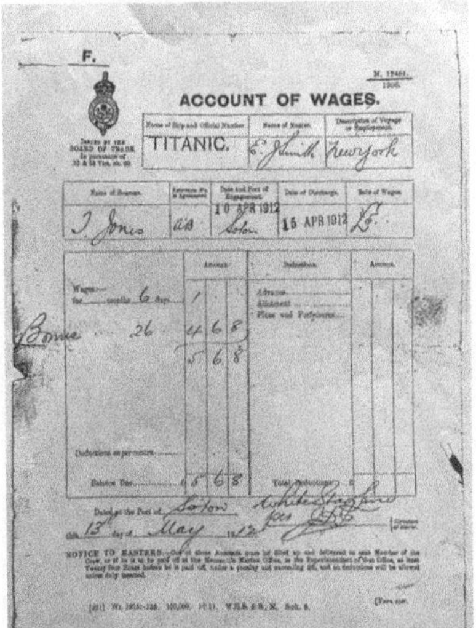

F.

ACCOUNT OF WAGES.

TITANIC.

10 APR 1912

15 APR 1912

The White Star Line did pay crew bonuses after *Titanic* sank. On 13 May 1912, Thomas Jones was paid £5 6*s* 8*d* (£3,800 in 2025). His six-day wage was £1 (£750 in 2025). His twenty-six-day bonus was £4 6*s* 8*d* (£3,050 in 2025). (Thomas Jones' Account of Wages, courtesy of Shelagh Oakes)

themselves, as were the scientists Louis Pasteur and Marie Curie; Henry Ford was designing his first cars; and the Wright Brothers were making their first attempts at flight. It was a time of growing availability of electric light and so, of course, it was the time of the cinema. Crucially for *Titanic*'s passengers and crew, it was the time when Guglielmo Marconi invented and patented wireless telegraphy. His invention was described as 'a system of transmitting messages between distant points *without the use of wires*' [my italics].[32] And then, just as now, it was the young who were fascinated by the new technology and quickly learnt how to operate it.

Titanic's chief Radio Operator, Jack Phillips, was just 25 (he had his twenty-fifth birthday on board *Titanic* on 11 April 1912); his assistant, Harold Bride, was 22. *Titanic*'s Marconi equipment was, according to Guglielmo Marconi:

> A fairly powerful set, capable, I should say, of communicating four or five hundred miles during the daytime and much further during the nighttime … very often a thousand miles … every night … with accuracy.[33]

And so it was that, in this era of invention and optimism, of possibility, of flourishing imaginations and multiplying inventions and,

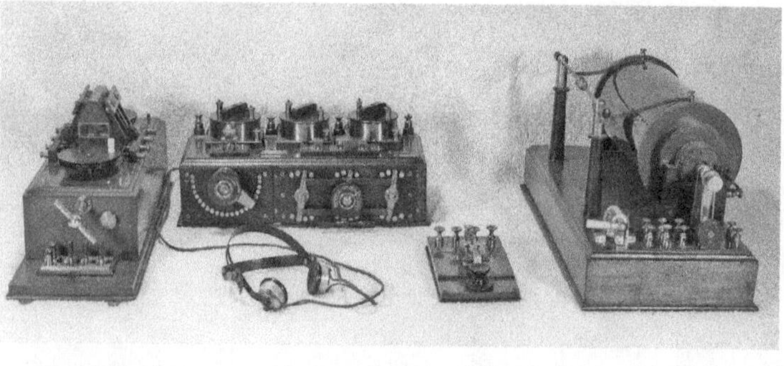

Original Marconi equipment restored by Linc Cundall, Antique Wireless Association Museum. (Image courtesy of the California Historical Radio Society and the Antique Wireless Association)

for many, a sense of invincibility coupled with an absolute faith in science and technology, the White Star Line published a brochure, in 1910, advertising their Olympic Class liners that included this striking sentence:

> As far as it is possible to do so, these two wonderful vessels [*Olympic* and *Titanic*] are designed to be unsinkable.[34]

Designed to be unsinkable. *Titanic*'s owners were convinced.

In an issue of *The Shipbuilder*, published in 1911, *Titanic*'s watertight doors are described as making 'the vessel practically unsinkable'.[35] And there is, gathered together in the *Titanic* historian and author George Behe's article, 'How the *Titanic* Became "Unsinkable"',[36] much evidence to show that *Titanic* was considered unsinkable by her owners, her designers, the crew and those about to travel on board. Certainly the White Star Line set great store by *Titanic*'s ability to act as 'a lifeboat in itself'.

The first four (and the last three) of her watertight compartments were designed to withstand a head-on collision; any two compartments were designed to withstand a side-on (amidships) collision; and she had a double bottom designed to contain flooding if she ran aground.[37] In 1909, when the White Star Liner, the *Republic*, was hit by another ship in thick fog and sank nine hours afterwards, all but six of the 1,500 people on board were transferred to other ships before she sank – ships that had picked up distress signals from the *Republic*'s Marconi room. It was one of the first marine rescues made possible by radio[38] and the young Marconi Operator, Jack Binns, became a hero.[39] When *Titanic*'s sister ship, the *Olympic*, collided with the Royal Navy ship, the *Hawke*, on 20 September 1911, her watertight apparatus operated exactly as it had been designed to: the watertight doors closed correctly and water in the two flooded compartments never spread any further. Unlike earlier ships, *Olympic* didn't sink; safety claims appeared to have been validated and so the 'unsinkable' legend of the White Star Line's Olympic Class liners was born.[40]

Captain Smith himself commented after the collision with the *Hawke* that 'The *Olympic* is unsinkable, and *Titanic* will be the same when she is put in commission.'[41] A caulker, a person responsible for making sure a ship is watertight, said:

> If you had seen or known the process of extra work that went into the ship, you'd say it was impossible to sink her.[42]

But, of course, it wasn't impossible to sink her.

When the iceberg scraped into her starboard hull, *six* of *Titanic*'s watertight compartments were flooded, five badly, and there was minor flooding to boiler room five's coal bunker. The American Inquiry's Final Report states:

> The 5 extreme forward compartments were flooded practically immediately, and under such circumstances, by reason of the non-watertight character of the deck at which the transverse bulkheads ended, the supposedly watertight compartments were NOT watertight, and the sinking of the vessel followed.[43]

Julian Fellowes, creator of the *Downton Abbey* and *Titanic* series, among others,[44] said only an iceberg – not another ship – could have caused that kind of damage.[45] Which suggests a failure of imagination on the part of *Titanic*'s owners and designers: they didn't anticipate needing to make her watertight against an iceberg that might cause a long thin gash along her hull.[46] Despite icebergs on the north Atlantic route.

But even as they were being ordered into the lifeboats, *Titanic*'s passengers were convinced she was unsinkable. They'd booked passage knowing that this brand-new ship was unlike any other ship in the world and that she'd been equipped with the best that contemporary shipbuilding technology could offer. They *knew* she couldn't sink. Among Noël's press cuttings is one from *The Daily Graphic* dated 30 April 1912. Two first-class stewardesses described why some women wouldn't board the lifeboats:

> Many more [women] could have been saved if the dangers had been realised earlier. The lady passengers preferred in the early stages to take their chance by remaining [on board *Titanic*] rather than get down into the boats – a terrifying experience to them.

In an interview written almost forty-four years after the disaster, on 15 March 1956, when interest in *Titanic* had revived after *A Night to Remember* was published, Thomas Jones was asked why more people hadn't come forward to board the lifeboats. He said:

> The answer is that they would not get into the boats. The night was so fine and the *Titanic* was so large that they did not think it possible she could go down. Time and time again I heard Captain Smith appealing to them to board the lifeboats, but they did not and the boats, in many cases, left half full.[47]

As news of the *Titanic*'s sinking began to reach New York on Monday, 15 April 1912, Philip A.S. Franklin, American Vice President of the International Mercantile Marine Company, owner of several shipping lines including the White Star Line, still believed she couldn't sink:

> During the entire day we considered the ship unsinkable, and it never entered our minds that there had been anything like a serious loss of life.[48]

In *A Night to Remember*, Walter Lord quotes Mrs Albert Caldwell asking a deck hand, as he carried luggage to *Titanic*'s cabins at Southampton, 'Is this ship really non-sinkable?'

'Yes, lady,' he answered. 'God Himself could not sink this ship.'[49]

But in the early morning of 15 April 1912, 1,496 people died when the *Titanic* sank. Confirmation of the tragedy reached New York as the day wore on, as Marconigrams were sent from the rescue ship, the *Carpathia*.

Titanic was not invincible.

She had not acted as a lifeboat in herself.

She *could* sink.

Afterwards, in his evidence to the American Inquiry, Able Seaman Thomas Jones confirmed what the crew had believed, until that night:

> Senator NEWLANDS: You thought the ship was unsinkable, did you?
> Mr. JONES: Yes, sir; I thought so.
> Senator NEWLANDS: Was that the view of the crew, generally?
> Mr. JONES: Yes, sir.[50]

Three

Luxury or Lifeboats

We all thought there were plenty of boats[1]

If you've seen James Cameron's 1997 film *Titanic*, you'll have seen a reproduction of the grand staircase in first class. In the White Star Line's brochure for *Titanic* and her sister ship *Olympic*, the staircase is described as:

> Sixteen feet wide, extend[ing] over sixty feet and serv[ing] seven decks … It is modelled closely after the style so prevalent during the reign of William and Mary, except that instead of the usual heavily-carved balustrade, a light wrought-iron grille has been employed, a fashion found in a few of the most exclusive great houses of that period. The Entrance Hall and Grand Staircase are surmounted by a glass dome of great splendour, a fitting crown … to these the largest and finest steamers in all the world.[2]

It sounds like the description of a grand staircase on land, and that was exactly the illusion *Titanic*'s owners wanted to create. A luxurious floating hotel. The staircase and many other saloons and fittings on board contributed to the passengers' difficulty in believing she might sink and so their reluctance to board the lifeboats.

The third-class stairwells were very different: they looked much like those in British cross-Channel ferries still look. The differences between these two stairwells graphically illustrates the differences between the privileged passengers in first class and the migrants in third class – between the wealthy Aristocrat travelling in luxury and the working Able Seaman.

Much has been written about *Titanic*'s designers *decreasing* the number of lifeboats their liners carried. But during the design process the number was actually *increased* (although the number of passengers was *decreased*). The maritime author and historian Mark Chirnside's research includes this table, which illustrates the changes.[3]

	'Design "D"' Proposal for *Olympic/Titanic* (1908)	*Titanic* (1912)	Difference
Passenger capacity	3,104	2,471	- 20.4%
Crew	875	944	+ 7.3%
Total passengers and crew	3,979	3,415	- 14.2%
Lifeboat Capacity	990	1,178	+ 19%
Lifeboat Capacity as Proportion of Ship's Capacity	24.9%	34.5%	+ 38.6%

Design for *Titanic*'s lifeboat capacity, showing (second column) an *increase* in capacity but a *decrease* in passenger capacity. Also showing an *increase* in crew capacity. (Image courtesy of Mark Chirnside first published in the British Titanic Society's *Atlantic Daily Bulletin*, September 2018)

However, despite the increase, *Titanic* set sail *without* enough lifeboats for all. In his talk, *Olympic and Titanic: A Very Remote Contingency*,[4] Chirnside discusses how, in the late 1880s, the British Board of Trade began to look at the out-of-date regulations for lifeboat provision. The emphasis, when thinking about saving life at sea, was still on the 'proper placing of bulkheads', but reform was on the way. The Merchant Shipping Act of 1894 (Lifeboat Amendment Act) required ships of '10,000 gross tons and above to carry sixteen lifeboats, and *if those boats didn't provide accommodation for everyone on board then additional lifeboats should be carried* [my italics]'.[5] And there was peer pressure from the White Star Line's rival, Cunard, who, by February 1912, had decided to fit 'boats for all' (lifeboats for every single human being on board) on their new liner, the *Aquitania*,[6] which launched in 1914. (If a ship's suffix was *-ic* it was a White Star Liner; if it was *-ia* it was a Cunarder.)

By 1908, ships of 45,000 tons (*Titanic* was 46,328 tons) were being built at Harland & Wolff, and Alexander Carlisle, *Titanic*'s chief designer, began thinking about changing the lifeboat arrangements for their Olympic Class ships. Carlisle opted for a better davit design, the Welin Davit, which could launch two lifeboats from the same one. But when *Titanic* sailed she only had one boat per davit (and it's true that it would have been difficult to get two boats per davit away in time). They also considered a lifeboat design that would have equipped *Titanic* with an outer set of sixteen lifeboats for sixty people each and an inner set of sixteen for fifty people each, for a total of 1,760: 582 more lifeboat places than the number she actually sailed with (1,178).

In the original design, the lifeboats were stowed on the first- and second-class promenade decks; in the final design, those to be stowed on the first-class promenade deck were moved to the officers' promenade deck. That gave first-class passengers much more room to walk and very likely fuelled the myth that Bruce Ismay turned down a design for more lifeboats because he didn't want them cluttering up the deck where his first-class passengers would want to stroll. And the fact that there were no lifeboats on

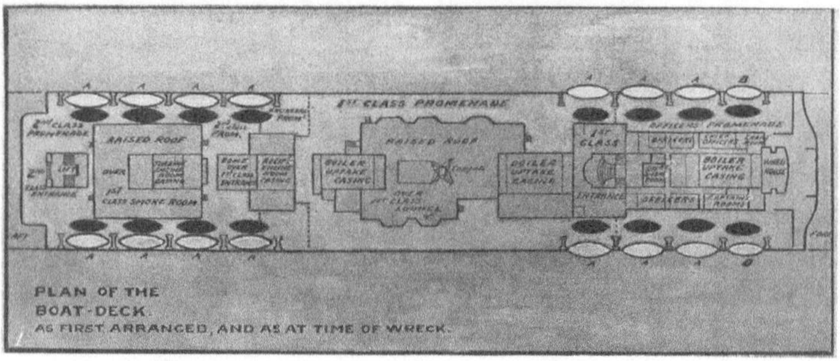

An early lifeboat quota: *Titanic* sailed *without* the black boats, and those on the officers' promenade deck were originally planned for the first-class deck. The final design gave first-class passengers much more room to walk. (Image: *Illustrated London News*, 1912. Courtesy of Mark Chirnside)

the first-class promenade deck meant there was nothing to 'spoil the view'.[7]

By the time Alexander Carlisle retired at the end of June 1910, no decision had been made about how many lifeboats *Titanic* would carry. She did, in the end, sail with sixteen lifeboats as the law required – the white boats in the illustration above. She also carried four extra Engelhardt collapsibles – not illustrated – making a total lifeboat capacity, in human terms, for 1,178 souls[8] (or 1,176, according to the American Inquiry, but I will use 1,178).[9] It was more than the legal requirement but, even if filled to capacity, those lifeboats would hold roughly 1,022 *fewer* passengers and crew than the actual number of people on board (2,208)[10] and roughly 2,237 fewer than the total number of people *Titanic* might have been carrying if she'd been filled to capacity (see the table on page 36).

One of the persistent rumours about *Titanic* is that her third-class passengers were kept away from the lifeboats. In the book *Report into the Loss of the SS Titanic*, the authors conclude that there isn't yet any concrete physical evidence of floor-to-ceiling gates inside *Titanic*'s wreck, but there is:

> Too much circumstantial evidence (passenger accounts, existing gates on her two sister ships etc.) for us to conclude that *Titanic* had no physical barriers that prevented at least some third class passengers from reaching the boat deck.[11]

There *were* barriers across the tops of the third-class stairwells (Lawrence Beesley wrote about 'low gates'); there were also gates across some corridors, but as John E. Hart, a third-class steward, said in his evidence to the British Inquiry, the barriers could be lifted by hand and they weren't locked. When he was asked if a third-class passenger could reach second- or first-class decks by pushing the gate or lifting the barrier, he said they could. But he also said:

> That is, of course, if there is nobody there on watch. There usually is a quartermaster standing by there or a seaman.[12]

Curious third-class passengers who wanted to see what the rest of the ship looked like would have been inhibited by whoever was on watch.

But the reason there were gates in the first place was *not* to stop third-class passengers from reaching the lifeboats, but to stop the spread of disease. The American Immigration Authorities conducted rigorous health checks at Ellis Island and any immigrant who failed the tests was sent back to Europe at the shipping company's expense, so, to mitigate that risk, companies kept their third-class passengers separate from those in first and second class,[13] because they believed that the largely migrant third class were more likely to carry and spread disease. The actual effect was tragic: 528 (of 709) third-class passengers died, while the total was 289 (of 608) for first and second class.[14]

Third-class quarters were the farthest away from the lifeboats. In the four and a half days before *Titanic* collided with the iceberg, first- and second-class passengers explored the ship; third class couldn't. But *Titanic*'s third-class accommodation was exceptionally good, so perhaps they didn't mind the lack of access to other decks. Until the night she collided with the iceberg.

The tragic consequence of the barriers and their guardians was that, after the collision, when the stewards began to tell third-class passengers where to go and what to do, many struggled to understand the instructions (approximately half weren't native English speakers); and, because they hadn't had a chance to explore the ship, they'd never been to the boat deck, so they didn't know where to go. Notices about how to get around the ship were only printed in English and there weren't anything like enough of them,[15] and although some of the stokers stayed below to maintain power so *Titanic*'s lights (and her Marconi equipment) stayed on, terrified third-class passengers had to navigate unknown territory.

John E. Hart said:

> It must have been three parts of an hour [after 11.40 p.m., the time *Titanic* collided with the iceberg] before the word was passed down to me to pass the [third-class] women and children up to the boat deck ... about 12.30.[16]

His orders came almost an hour after the collision, at about the same time Noël said hers came. But Hart also said a number of women refused to go up to the boat deck because they felt safer in their warm, dry quarters:

> I heard two or three say they preferred to remain on the ship than be tossed about on the water like a cockle shell.[17]

Senator William Alden Smith said that aft steerage (third class):

> Was a deck higher than the forward steerage, and was lifted higher and higher until the ship finally disappeared – [aft] steerage passengers got their first warning of real danger as the angle of the deck became very great. I feel that the small number of steerage survivors was thus due to the fact that they got no definite warning before the ship was really doomed, when most of the lifeboats had departed.[18]

Had there been a lifeboat drill aboard *Titanic* before the collision, many more third-class passengers might have survived, at least among the women and children, because each member of the crew would have known which lifeboat number was assigned to him and might have boarded passengers more efficiently. In those days safety drills on board ship didn't involve passengers, they were only for the crew. Four surviving crew members said they'd expected a boat muster on Sunday, 14 April, but the orders never came, so when they made for their places to lower and man the lifeboats as *Titanic* began to sink, they had to rely on their memories for the boat number each was assigned when they left Southampton. The alternative was to go down to the galley where the lifeboat list was published, which was 'a risky thing to do' because water was already flooding in. One steward did go down and fixed his lifeboat number in his mind along with the numbers assigned to some of his mates in case he should see them.[19]

Alfred Crawford, a first-class bedroom steward who survived in Thomas Jones' Lifeboat Number 8, told the American Inquiry there was a safety drill on board *Titanic* in Belfast[20] *before* she set sail for Southampton. And there was (see page 15) a second drill involving two lifeboats at Southampton. But because there were no drills while *Titanic* was at sea, the crew weren't adequately prepared for a total evacuation. In his concluding speech to the American Inquiry, Senator William Alden Smith said:

> No drill or station practice or helpful discipline disturbed the tranquillity of that voyage, and when the crisis came a state of absolute unpreparedness stupefied both passengers and crew.[21]

The policy of women and children first into the lifeboats meant that many more women and children from all passenger classes and crew survived than men but, even so, if third-class passengers hadn't been kept to their quarters and if the class system hadn't been so rigid that they didn't attempt to climb over the low gates, many more third-class women and children could have survived.

However ... *Titanic* sailed without *enough* lifeboats for every human being on board because the British Board of Trade's calculation for lifeboat requirements in those days was based on a ship's tonnage or size, *not* on the potential numbers of human beings on board. And the Merchant Shipping Act in force at the time had a fatal flaw: the tonnage for calculating the number of lifeboats stood at 10,000 tons.[22] *Titanic*'s gross registered tonnage was 46,328 tons. If Maritime Law had kept pace with early twentieth-century technological and shipbuilding advances, and if *Titanic*'s owners and designers had followed the Law's own guidance to provide lifeboat accommodation for everyone on board if the sixteen required didn't, she would have carried enough lifeboats for every single soul on board.

The real issue, as Mark Chirnside points out, is that boats for *everyone* weren't required at the time; the emphasis for safety at sea was still on watertight bulkhead provision. Arthur Rostron, *Carpathia*'s Captain, said:

> Ships are built nowadays to be practically unsinkable, and *each ship is supposed to be a lifeboat in itself* [my italics]. The [life]boats are merely supposed to be put on as a standby.[23]

That was also the view of Sir Alfred Chalmers, an experienced master mariner and technical advisor to the Marine Department at the UK's Board of Trade between 1877 and 1911. He said to the British Inquiry into the disaster:

> As ships grew bigger, there were such improvements made in their construction that they were stronger and better ships, both from the point of view of watertight compartments and also absolute strength ... . I [also] considered from my experience that [sixteen lifeboats together with supplementary boats] was the maximum number that could be rapidly dealt with at sea and that would be safely housed without encumbering the vessel's decks unduly.[24]

The second-class promenade deck with one row of lifeboats; an earlier design had two rows. More boats would have saved more lives, assuming the extra boats could have been lowered in the short time before *Titanic* sank. (Smith Archive/ Alamy Stock Photo)

I very much doubt there were any women on the Board of Trade[25] in the early twentieth century but I wish there had been, because a woman's perspective can be different from a man's. If there had been women on the Board I think it's safe to say that they would have made sure any lifeboat calculation for passenger liners was based on the potential numbers of human beings on board, not on a mathematical calculation that used the size, or tonnage, of a ship, *however* safe those liners were thought to be. I also think it's safe to say that if women had been in charge when the Board was thinking about the safety of human life at sea, they would've been less convinced by the idea that a ship, however technologically advanced, was unlikely to sink. They'd have been more humble about the idea that anything designed by human beings could defy the elements. I like to think – had any women earned their place on the Board – that they'd have done their best to make sure there were 'boats for everyone' and brooked no argument.

But I do accept that it might have been difficult to load more lifeboats in the short time between *Titanic*'s collision with the iceberg and the time she sank. Although, at the time, the seas were as full of shipping as our skies are full of aircraft now, so there was a failsafe: if a ship got into trouble her crew would send distress signals, confident in the knowledge that a nearby ship, or several ships, would respond. The able seamen would lower away the lifeboats filled with passengers and crew and ferry them from the ship in trouble to other ship(s). Once they'd ferried all the passengers and crew to other ships, the ship in trouble would be left with a skeleton crew who'd either work out how to solve the problem, or disembark for the other ship(s) if the problem proved insoluble.

Lifeboats in those days were thought of as ferries. They were never expected to act as life savers on their own. And that's why ships sailed safely (their owners thought) without enough lifeboats for every single human on board. If a ferrying process had happened on the night *Titanic* collided with the iceberg, it's possible many more passengers and crew could have been saved. Able Seaman Thomas Jones expected to ferry his passengers in Lifeboat Number 8 to another ship:

> He [the Captain] told me to row for the light [of a ship] and land the passengers and return to the ship.[26]

Noël also recorded the Captain's order in one of the press cuttings found after she died:

> Captain Smith stood shoulder to shoulder with me as I got into the life boat, and his last words were to the lone seaman – Tom Jones – 'Row straight for those ship lights over there: leave your passengers on board of her and return as soon as you can.' Captain Smith's whole attitude was one of great calmness and courage, and I am sure he thought that the ship – whose lights we could plainly see – would pick us up and that our life

> boats would be able to do double duty in ferrying passengers to the help that gleamed so near.[27]

Smith confidently expected the ferrying process to succeed. The reason it didn't was, although the Captain of the ship Smith saw could see *Titanic*, that ship's Captain wasn't sure *Titanic was Titanic* and never responded to her distress rockets (see Chapter Five).

Just two weeks after *Titanic* sank, the White Star Line added forty collapsible boats to *Olympic*'s lifeboat quota, but many of them were thought unseaworthy by the crewmen, who went on strike and refused to sail until better-quality boats were installed.[28] Between 1912 and 1913, when *Olympic* was refitted, her lifeboat capacity was increased from twenty to sixty-eight, implying, I think, that the White Star Line knew very well, after *Titanic*, that twenty lifeboats wasn't anything like enough. See the table below.[29]

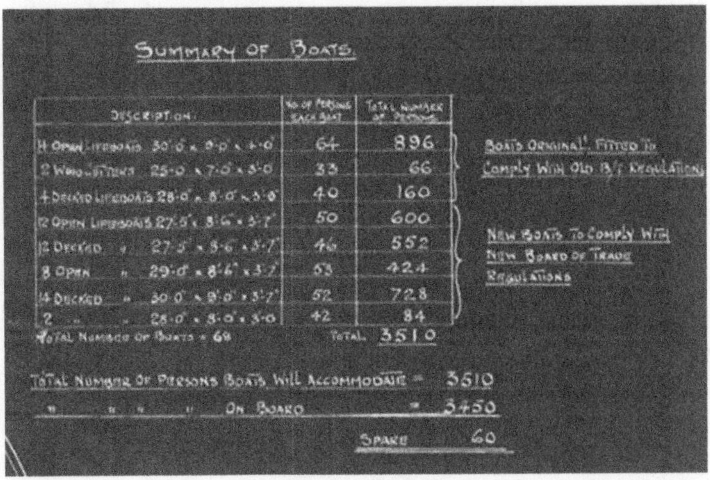

SUMMARY OF BOATS.

DESCRIPTION.	No. OF PERSONS EACH BOAT	TOTAL NUMBER OF PERSONS	
14 OPEN LIFEBOATS 30·0 × 9·0 × 4·0	64	896	BOATS ORIGINALLY FITTED TO COMPLY WITH OLD B/T REGULATIONS
2 WOOD CUTTERS 25·0 × 7·0 × 3·0	33	66	
4 DECKED LIFEBOATS 28·0 × 8·0 × 3·0	40	160	
12 OPEN LIFEBOATS 27·5 × 8·6 × 3·7	50	600	NEW BOATS TO COMPLY WITH NEW BOARD OF TRADE REGULATIONS
12 DECKED " 27·5 × 8·6 × 3·7	46	552	
8 OPEN " 29·0 × 8·6 × 3·7	53	424	
14 DECKED " 30·0 × 8·0 × 3·7	52	728	
2 " " 28·0 × 8·0 × 3·0	42	84	
TOTAL NUMBER OF BOATS = 68	TOTAL	3510	

TOTAL NUMBER OF PERSONS BOATS WILL ACCOMMODATE = 3510
" " " " ON BOARD = 3450
SPARE 60

The large increase in lifeboat capacity on *Olympic* after the *Titanic* disaster. In 1912, *Titanic* sailed with twenty lifeboats. In 1913, *Olympic* sailed with sixty-eight, in anticipation of the new Board of Trade regulations. (February 1913 Blueprint, courtesy of Mark Chirnside)

In her letter to her parents, Noël wrote:

> We all thought there were plenty of boats – little knowing that there were only 16.[30]

With the four Engelhardt collapsibles there were twenty lifeboats, but Noël was right: there were only sixteen wooden boats.

In his evidence to the American Inquiry, Bruce Ismay admitted he gave instructions – two days after he disembarked the *Carpathia* in New York on 20 April 1912 – that no ship belonging to the International Mercantile Marine Company was to leave port unless she had 'sufficient boats on board for the accommodation of all the passengers and the whole of the crew'.[31] This instruction implies Ismay's anxiety: no ship belonging to the company was ever to set out again without enough lifeboats for every single soul on board. It also implies he knew he'd made a grave mistake when he believed *Titanic* had been built to be 'a lifeboat in itself'. She needed more lifeboats, just as the White Star Line's rivals, Cunard, planned for the *Aquitania* (see page 37).

Titanic had fifteen watertight bulkheads: eight reached D Deck and seven reached E Deck, but they proved too low when the iceberg scraped along her starboard hull (it was neither a head-on nor an amidships collision) and the watertight compartments were breached. The ship was designed to withstand flooding in any two or three compartments and 'in some scenarios with four flooded'.[32] Six was two too many and the bulkheads acted like giant jam jars or giant ice cube trays: water poured over the top of one into the next and the next and the next.

The White Star Line's desire to make its first-class passengers believe they were travelling in a luxurious palace, a floating hotel, meant, in the end, that their safety was unwittingly sacrificed for luxury and so very many of them paid for that luxury with their lives. If the bulkheads had been taller they'd have reduced space in the saloons, but the flooding would have been contained.

The American Inquiry found that:

> The openings through deck E were not designed for watertight closing ... the evidence shows that flooding over deck E contributed largely to the sinking of vessel.[33]

Mark Chirnside points out that the Senators who conducted the American Inquiry weren't naval architects and that the fundamental reason *Titanic* sank was that too many watertight compartments were flooded, not that her bulkheads failed to act as they were designed to act. Bruce Ismay was asked if he thought a collision that flooded two watertight compartments would be the most serious damage *Titanic* was likely to face. He said it was and that they'd provided against it.[34] But six forward compartments were flooded almost immediately.

Some believe only a head-on collision could have prevented *Titanic* sinking[35] because although her bow would have been crushed, fewer watertight compartments would have been breached. But human beings naturally try to avoid collisions that might kill. A head-on collision with the iceberg would have killed all those in the forward berths: the off-shift engineers and the single men travelling third class. Some also say poor riveting caused her to sink, but although a few rivets taken from the wreck have shown high levels of sulphurous slag, which, at low temperatures, might have made them more brittle, *Olympic*'s long career and *Titanic*'s wreck today demonstrate that the majority of rivets and metalwork were perfectly strong.[36]

So, not enough lifeboats, too many holed watertight compartments and the fact that eight lifeboats left *Titanic* with fewer than fifty people on board – expecting to carry out a ferrying process that never happened – contributed to the tragic number of deaths, particularly among the men, so many of whom obeyed the request to stand back so that the women and children could board the lifeboats first.

Four

Leaving *Titanic*

I pulled for the light, and I found that I could not get near the light[1]

Titanic collided with the iceberg at 11.40 p.m. on Sunday, 14 April 1912, three days before she should have arrived in New York. Many passengers were asleep or getting ready for bed; those who were still awake noticed what Lawrence Beesley described as 'nothing more than an extra heave of the engines'.[2] In a *New York Herald* article dated 22 April 1912, one of those found with her *Titanic* papers, Noël described noticing 'a slight jar and then a grating noise'. She said, 'I turned on the light and saw that it was 11.46 and I wondered at the sudden quiet.'[3] By contrast, Marie Grice Young, a first-class passenger who also survived in Lifeboat Number 8, described it as 'a grinding wrenching force followed by several violent bumps'.[4]

The crew and passengers on the lower, forward starboard decks heard and saw much more than the crew and the first- and second-class passengers on higher decks. Dr Rudi Newman writes:

> Fourth Officer Boxhall was walking along the starboard A Deck and the collision did not even interrupt his stride, despite the iceberg reaching up to the boat deck 60 feet above

> the water. Thomas Andrews [who'd been on board since Southampton] was working in his cabin and failed to notice the collision ... [but] in third class and the crew's quarters the ship shook and people were thrown out of bed.[5]

The order for the deck crew to uncover the boats came at about midnight, twenty minutes after the collision. The order to get women and children up to the boat deck came about forty-five minutes after the collision when Thomas Andrews, who'd been below to assess the damage, thought the ship had from an hour to an hour and a half left. She actually stayed afloat for almost two more hours.[6]

Mrs J. Stuart White, another survivor in Lifeboat Number 8, said:

> It did not seem to me that there was any very great impact at all. It was just as though we went over about a thousand marbles.[7]

But Gladys Cherry wrote to her mother on 17 April 1912:

> Noël and I ... were awakened by an awful sort of bang and the engines stopping suddenly, we had an extraordinary feeling that something dreadful had happened as, when the engines stopped there was a terrible silence then the awful noise of steam being let off.[8]

The third-class forward passengers, according to Senator Smith:

> Knew directly of the impact and of the presence of water, which came up from the lower part of the ship into the mail room and the forward steerage.[9]

There was a dramatic difference between what forward and aft third-class passengers saw and heard: the former saw flooding early so they were more willing to go up to the boat deck when the stewards called them; the latter never saw any flooding so they were more reluctant to leave the ship. But passengers in all classes felt no sense of urgency even if they had seen flooding because they *knew* *Titanic* was unsinkable.

Lawrence Beesley wrote about the moment *Titanic* collided with the iceberg (he didn't know that that was what it was at the time):

> [There was] a more than usually obvious dancing motion of the mattress … . Nothing more than that – no sound of a crash or of anything else … . [But] all this time the *Titanic* was being cut open by the iceberg and water was pouring in her side … . [There was] no cry in the night; no alarm given; no one afraid … . But in a few moments I felt the engines slow and stop … the dancing motion and the vibration ceased suddenly after being part of our very existence for four days, and that was the first hint that anything out of the ordinary had happened.[10]

In one of Noël's press cuttings, from *The Daily Telegraph* on 20 April 1912, Mrs J.J. Brown, wife of a Denver mine owner, later known as the 'Unsinkable Molly Brown', is quoted:

> It was all so formal it was difficult for anyone to realise it was a tragedy. Men and women stood in little groups and talked and laughed.

Noël agreed about the lack of panic, the sense that nothing serious had happened. In her sworn statement to the British Vice-Consul in Altadena she said:

> On opening my cabin door, I saw the steward who attended my cabin, and upon asking him what had occurred, was informed that the ship had been in collision with ice. As we wished to see an iceberg, we went on deck and walked to the forward part where we could see the portion of the boat occupied by steerage passengers. The deck below was covered with ice, but we did not see the iceberg.

> There was no disturbance or confusion among the passengers.[11]

Alfred Crawford said he heard a crash and went out 'on the outer deck'. He said he saw the iceberg 'going by',[12] but he reassured his passengers he didn't think there was any immediate danger. At first, very few people had any idea that the iceberg had fatally damaged *Titanic*. Gladys Cherry, in her letter to her mother, wrote about 'the perfect confidence the people had in that great boat', and:

> When we reached the water I felt we had done a foolish thing to leave that big safe boat, but when we had rowed a few yards, we saw that great ship with her bows right down in the water.[13]

In her letter to her parents Noël wrote:

> We struck the iceberg at quarter to 12 on Sunday night. At first, and until nearly one o'clock, no one realised any danger – or really knew what had happened – then the order came to be dressed & have lifebelts on, in ten minutes – & we were then put into the life boats at quarter to 2 .... I just had time to pour out some brandy, give her some [Maioni, her ladies' maid], & Gladys & myself & hurriedly dress – then no-one seemed to know where the lifebelts were kept, & a strange man found ours for us – we then tied on his for him – & all shook hands & told each other that it would not be long before we met again.[14]

In a letter to her cousin and lifelong friend May Goodman, written from the safety of New York, Noël said that when they boarded the lifeboat they lost *everything* except the few clothes and fur coats they had time to put on. But she said, 'Luckily too for us lifebelts are warm things.'[15]

Both Noël and Gladys reported the 'appalling' and 'awful' noise of steam as it was released through the funnels: Noël, in her letter to

Walter Lord, in 1955 and Gladys, in the first letter she wrote to her mother, in 1912. The noise made communication between the crew difficult – they had to use sign language – and there were reports of gunshots when the last lifeboats, the Engelhardt collapsibles, were being loaded. Noël described, in an interview in the *Los Angeles Examiner* of 16 May 1912 – another of the press cuttings found with her *Titanic* papers – that as the great ship sank, her 'exploding boilers' made terrible reports. They 'sang a requiem' for the men left behind. What Noël thought were exploding boilers were 'undoubtedly the thunderous sounds caused by the ship breaking in two',[16] George Behe told me. And Dr Rudi Newman wrote that the sounds were the boilers *imploding*.[17] Alfred Crawford heard sharp explosions, 'as if things were being blown up'.[18] But when Robert Ballard and Jean-Louis Michel found the wreck of the *Titanic* on the seabed in 1985, they discovered that the ship's boilers were intact and had not exploded (see page 139). What Noël and others thought were exploding boilers were more likely to have been machinery crashing through the ship and/or the steel of the ship ripping and tearing as *Titanic*'s bow tipped and her stern lifted, causing the hull to break in two,[19] as George Behe said.

Sound travels well across water and those lucky enough to have found a place in a lifeboat heard the terrible screams and cries for help from people struggling in the freezing water behind them, as *Titanic* sank. Fifth Officer Lowe said he fired 'three shots' to prevent any more people boarding his already crowded lifeboat, Number 14. He said he fired:

> Without intention of hurting anybody and also with the knowledge that I did not hurt anybody [he fired horizontally] … between the boat and the ship's side, so these people [who Lowe feared would jump into his lifeboat from the open decks] would hear and see the discharge.[20]

Lowe's lifeboat was one of the last to leave *Titanic*, at about 1.30 a.m., so those in the boats that left earlier probably wouldn't have heard his warning shots. Nor would they have heard the shots fired by another officer; it isn't known which officer, but two different survivor letters record that an unnamed officer took his own life with a revolver during *Titanic*'s last moments afloat.[21]

Able Seaman Thomas Jones was ordered to command Lifeboat Number 8. His boat was the second to leave *Titanic*'s port side at 1.10 a.m., according to the British Inquiry. But before its list of lifeboat launch times[22] there's this caveat:

> So far as can be ascertained the boats left the ship at the following times, but I [Lord Mersey, the British Wreck Commissioner][23] think it is necessary to say that these, and, indeed, all the times subsequent to the collision which are mentioned by the witnesses, are unreliable.

One of those witness reports was made by Noël. In her letter to her parents she said Lifeboat Number 8 left *Titanic*'s side at 1.45 a.m., more than half an hour after the British Inquiry recorded it leaving. But a couple of long paragraphs later Noël writes, 'We got into the boat a little before 1.30.'[24] There's no record that Noël was wearing a watch that night but, even if she was, at a time of great anxiety and fear it's hardly surprising she recorded times that differed from the official ones, although if she *boarded* the boat at 1.30 a.m. and Lifeboat Number 8 left *Titanic*'s side at 1.45 a.m., that would make sense.

It's also hardly surprising that many of the witness reports about the times the boats left the ship were 'unreliable'. Whatever the exact time, the boat commanded by Thomas Jones that Noël Rothes survived in was among the first to leave *Titanic*. Caroline Bonnell, another of Lifeboat Number 8's survivors, wrote, 'The boat we were in was the second to be let down over the side but the first to strike water,'[25] but in a careful revision of the lifeboat launch times, using evidence that wasn't available in 1912, Bill Wormstedt, Tad Fitch and George Behe have compiled a list that shows Lifeboat Number 8 was the fourth to leave and the first from the port side, at 1 a.m.[26]

Lifeboat Number 6 approaching the *Carpathia*. Captain Rostron suggested his friend, Louis Mansfield Ogden (d.1946), document the arrival of *Titanic*'s survivors with his new camera. From Rostron's 1931 book, *Home from the Sea*. (Image courtesy of Michael Pocock and Maritime Quest)

In his evidence to the American Inquiry, when asked about the number of people in his lifeboat, Thomas Jones said:

> I had 35 ladies and one sailor besides myself, and two stewards.[27]

The other sailor was Able Seaman Charles Pascoe. The two stewards were bedroom steward Alfred Crawford, and a cook or scullion (washer-up), probably Alfred Simmons. Alfred Crawford said there were about thirty-five people in Lifeboat Number 8 and two sailors.[28] He also said there were between thirty-five and forty.[29] In Noël Rothes' sworn statement she said there were 'about thirty others', and Caroline Bonnell said there were 'but twenty women, two sailors and a steward'.[30]

Differing records, including Noël's own, give differing numbers of people in Lifeboat Number 8 and (see page 14) *Titanic*'s passenger and crew lists were not accurate at the time because of misspellings, omissions, aliases and other mistakes. In her letter to her parents, Noël wrote that there were twenty-four women in Lifeboat Number 8, two stewards and one seaman; that letter was written on 18 April 1912, much closer to *Titanic*'s sinking than her sworn statement, given in May 1912. Gladys Cherry confirmed the same numbers in her letter to her mother, also written on board the *Carpathia* a day earlier than Noël's letter, on 17 April. An *Encyclopedia Titanica* list of those on board Lifeboat Number 8 states there were 'probably about twenty-six';[31] the British Wreck Commission says there were thirty-nine;[32] but a 2025 study, mostly based on first-hand accounts, suggests twenty-seven. Two of those on board aren't confirmed,[33] but perhaps that study will eventually identify a definitive, accurate number. What is accurate is that Lifeboat Number 8 could have taken sixty-five people, but she left *Titanic* less than half full. If she'd left fully loaded she might have saved the lives of thirty, perhaps even thirty-eight, more people.

Even-numbered lifeboats were stowed on *Titanic*'s port side; uneven on the starboard side. Second Officer Lightoller was in charge of boarding the boats on the port side and he interpreted 'women and children first' as women and children only.[34] First Officer Murdoch, who was in charge of boarding lifeboats on the starboard side, interpreted the command more leniently: if a lifeboat had filled with as many women and children as he could find, he allowed the waiting men to board.[35] Lightoller's strict interpretation meant fewer men survived, but 'women and children first' was never written into Maritime Law – it was the result of what became known as the Birkenhead Drill. When HM Troopship *Birkenhead* hit an uncharted rock on 26 February 1852 she began to sink quickly. Her passengers – reinforcement troops for the final stages of the Xhosa Wars – were told to stand fast so that twenty-six women and children, the servicemen's families, could board the *Birkenhead*'s cutter. The women and children were all saved but the men were not: they stood in rank as their ship sank and afterwards the Birkenhead Drill became common practice at sea.[36]

Thomas Jones reported that Captain Smith called for more ladies but when none came he ordered him to lower Lifeboat Number 8 away. Jones confidently expected to carry out the ferrying process described in Chapter Three. In his evidence to the American Inquiry he confirmed that his lifeboat could have taken sixty-five people. Then he said:

> [The Captain] told me to row for the light, and land the passengers and return to the ship. I pulled for the light, and I found that I could not get near the light, and I stood by for a little while. I wanted to return to the ship, but the ladies were frightened, and I had to carry out the Captain's orders and pull for that light; so I did so .... I thought they were only sending us away for an hour or so, until they got squared up again .... Until they got her pumped out.[37]

Alfred Crawford confirmed that they pulled and pulled for the light but they couldn't 'reach the ship'.[38] He said he saw two lights, not farther away than 10 miles. (To the British Inquiry he said the lights were between 5 and 7 miles away.)[39] The best recent estimate of that ship's distance from *Titanic* is between 12 and 14 miles north-north-west (magnetic).[40] Crawford said:

> They were stationary masthead lights, one on the fore and one on the main. Everybody saw them – all the ladies in the boat. They asked if we were drawing nearer to the steamer, but we could not seem to make any headway .... I am sure it was a steamer, because a sailing ship would not have two masthead lights.[41]

> ... Sometimes she seemed to get closer; other times she seemed to be getting away from us.[42] [And to both Inquiries, he said:] She seemed to be stationary.[43]

Mrs J. Stuart White confirmed that everyone in Lifeboat Number 8 saw the light. She also said, 'We all supposed that boat was coming toward us, on account of all the rockets that we had sent up.'[44] But one of the reasons Thomas Jones 'could not get near the light' was that he was trying to pull north against the Labrador Current, which pulls south-south-west.

In Noël's interview with the *Los Angeles Examiner*, on 16 May 1912, she said:

> Some [in Lifeboat Number 8] looked back to the great steamer which had been our ocean home; others peered ahead at the stern light of the steamer which knew or cared not of our peril. I can still see that stern light dimming, dimming, dimming until blackness came. Oh, that heartrending thought – we were alone on the ocean ... .
>
> The end? Oh, I could not look. Some of those in our boat peered at the dying vessel, with half averted faces, for they knew what her going down meant. There were women with us who had husbands, sons, brothers and other male kin on that ship. They knew the exploding boilers [*Titanic* breaking apart] sang a requiem [for them].[45]

When they reached the safety of New York, Noël gave an interview to *The New York Herald*. She gave it reluctantly as she heartily disapproved of the press' insatiable hunger for *Titanic* stories. But I think my great-grandmother wanted to tell the truth about what she'd witnessed to counteract press exaggerations and, perhaps especially, to tell the truth for the sake of all those who'd died.

This press cutting was one of the many found among her *Titanic* papers; extracts from it appear throughout the book. It was syndicated so there are several editions, including the European, Paris, edition and the New York edition.[46] What follows is the New York edition; it's slightly longer than the Paris edition but both were published on 22 April 1912. The original interview took place at the Ritz-Carlton hotel, although Noël and her husband were staying at the Plaza.

New York Herald, Monday April 22 1912

Lady Rothes Describes the Horror of Survivors' Chase of Phantom Light

'Rowing, Rowing Toward Beacon that Disappeared in the Night,' she says.

'The pitiful sadness of our rowing, rowing towards the lights of a ship that disappeared. We in boat No. 8 saw some tramp steamer's masthead lights, and then we saw the glow of red as she swung towards us for a few minutes. Then darkness and despair.'

Lady Rothes yesterday, at the Ritz Carlton, told of her experiences on board the *Titanic*.

'I went to bed at half-past seven,' she said, 'and my cousin, Miss Gladys Cherry, who shared my room – No. 77 on deck B – also retired. [Their cabin was on No. 77 on C Deck. And Gladys Cherry says, in one of her letters to her mother, that they went to bed at 10 p.m.] It was bitter cold. I was awakened by a slight jar and then a grating noise. I turned on the light and saw that it was 11:46 and I wondered at the sudden quiet. Gladys had not been awakened and I called her and asked did she not think it strange that the engines had stopped. As I opened our cabin door I saw a steward. He said we had struck some ice. Our fur coats over our night gowns were all the clothes we had. My cousin asked the chief steward if there was any danger and he answered, "Oh no, we have just grazed some ice and it does not amount to anything".'

The Call for Lifebelts

'As we hurried along Lambert Williams [a first-class passenger] came up and explained that the watertight compartments must surely hold. Just then an officer hurried by.

'"Will you get lifebelts on! Dress warmly and come up to A Deck!" Quite stunned by the order, we all went. As I was going in to our stateroom my maid said water was pouring into the racquet court. I gave her some brandy, tied on her lifebelt and told her to go straight up on deck. We had to ask a steward where our lifebelts could be found. The man said he was sure they were unnecessary until we told him we had been ordered to do so.

'We dressed as warmly as we could and went up to A deck. Mr Brown, the purser, touched his hat as we passed saying: – "It is quite all right: don't hurry!" What a lovely night it was! I stood close to Mrs Astor. She was waiting under the starboard ports [sic] of the library and her husband got a chair for her. She was quite calm. The last I saw of Colonel Astor was when he still stood by his wife, trying to comfort her.

'Captain Smith stood shoulder to shoulder with me as I got into the life boat, and his last words were to the lone seaman – Tom Jones – "Row straight for those ship lights over there: leave your passengers on board of her and return as soon as you can." Captain Smith's whole attitude was one of great calmness and courage, and I am sure he thought that the ship – whose lights we could plainly see – would pick us up and that our life boats would be able to do double duty in ferrying passengers to the help that gleamed so near.

'There were two stewards in boat No. 8 with us and thirty-one women. The name of the steward was Crawford. We were lowered quietly to the water, and when we had pushed off from the *Titanic*'s side I asked the seaman [Thomas Jones] if he would care to have me take the tiller, as I knew something about boats. He said, "Certainly, lady". I climbed aft into the stern sheets and asked my cousin to help me.

'The first impression I had as we left the ship was that above all things we must not lose our self-control. We had no officer to take command of our boat, and the little seaman had to assume all the responsibility. He did it nobly, alternately cheering us with words of encouragement, then rowing doggedly. Then Signora de Satode Peñasco began to scream for her husband. It was too horrible. I left the tiller to my cousin and slipped down beside her to be of what comfort I could. Poor woman! Her sobs tore our hearts and her moans were unspeakable in their sadness. Miss Cherry stayed at the tiller of our boat until the *Carpathia* picked us up.

'The most awful part of the whole thing was seeing the rows of portholes vanishing one by one. Several of us – and Tom Jones – wanted to row back and see if there was not some chance of rescuing any one that had possibly survived, but the majority in the boat ruled that we had no right to risk their lives on the bare chance of finding any one alive after the final plunge. They also said that the Captain's own orders had been to, "Row for those ship lights over there", and that we who wished to try for others who might be drowning had no business to interfere with his orders. Of course that settled the matter, and we rowed on.

'Indeed, I saw – we all saw – a ship's lights not more than three miles away!'

Turning to Lord Rothes, Lady Rothes said: – 'I am a fair judge of distances, am I not?' He answered, 'Yes, you are.'

The Lights Disappear

Continuing, Lady Rothes said: –

'For three hours we pulled steadily for the two masthead lights that showed brilliantly in the darkness. For a few minutes we saw the ship's port light, then it vanished, and the masthead lights got dimmer on the horizon until they, too, disappeared.

'A Mrs Smith [Swift] did yeoman service. She rowed for five hours with Tom Jones without taking a rest. Really, she was magnificent, not only in her attitude, but in the whole-souled way in which she worked.

'Mrs Pearson [Pears] also rowed, and my maid, Roberta Maioni, rowed the last half of the night.

'I did not know Mr Ismay by sight, until one night at dinner in the restaurant he came in late, and some one pointed him out to me as being the managing director of the line. There was no excitement of any kind, save that once the third class passengers became obstreperous, but it was instantly put down.' [In the Paris edition Noël is less harsh about the third-class passengers: 'A slight disturbance among the third-class passengers was at once quieted … .' She also said she didn't hear any shots.]

'When the awful end came, I tried my best to keep the Spanish woman from hearing the agonising sounds of distress. They seemed to continue forever, although it could not have been more than ten minutes until the silence of a lonely sea dropped down. The indescribable loneliness, the ghastliness of our feelings never can be told. We tried to keep in touch with the other boats by shouting, and succeeded fairly well. Our boat was the furthest away because we had chased the phantom lights for three hours. Yes, I rowed for three hours.'

Roberta Maioni, the maid, said: –

'I was not at all frightened. Everybody was saying as we left the ship that she was, "Good for twelve hours yet", and I was too numb to realise the terror of it all until we were safe on board the *Carpathia*.'

'Brave men all,' concluded the countess, 'that stood back so that the women should have at least a chance to live. Their memories should be held sacred in the mind of the world forever.'

Five

A Fatal Mistake

She was more of a man than any we had on board ... I put her at the tiller[1]

The steamship lights the passengers in Lifeboat Number 8 could see were those of the SS *Californian*. She was, it's now known, between 12 and 14 miles north-north-west (magnetic) of *Titanic* and by far the closest ship.[2] But the most important reason, with far more tragic consequences, that Jones couldn't 'get near' her lights was that the *Californian*'s Captain, Stanley Lord, made a fatal mistake. Even though his Apprentice Officer, James Gibson, told the British Inquiry he saw white rockets being fired to the south and reported them to his Captain, his Captain gave him no instructions.[3] But according to the British Board of Trade rulebook, if there's any doubt about a rocket's meaning it *must* be taken for a distress signal. That rule was ignored by the *Californian*'s Captain.[4]

Many survivors reported that it was a particularly clear, starry night, but what they didn't know was that the weather conditions that night were very unusual. Author, historian and TV presenter Tim Maltin's research has shown that an atmospheric phenomenon called thermal inversion (cold air trapped by the icebergs underneath warm air) caused an abnormal refraction of light that distorted

Captain Stanley Lord, Captain of the SS *Californian*. If he'd woken his Marconi Operator when he couldn't interpret the signals he saw, when he didn't realise *Titanic* was *Titanic*, it's possible that 100 extra lives – or more – could have been saved. (GL Archive/Alamy Stock Photo)

visibility. It made *Titanic*'s distress rockets appear lower and smaller than they really were to the crew of the *Californian*. It also made the distance between the two ships seem much less than it actually was to those in Lifeboat Number 8 and created a false horizon, an apparently raised horizon that looked real. This false horizon camouflaged part of the iceberg, reducing its apparent size and making it visible a few moments later than it would have been in normal refracting conditions.[5] Maltin writes:

> The unusually high eye-heights of the observers on … *Titanic*'s bridge and crow's nest … increased the dip of the horizon, thus putting the icebergs even farther below the false horizon … [making] the icebergs at *Titanic*'s crash site impossible to detect until it was too late to avoid a collision.[6]

Titanic's lookouts reported a haze all around the horizon – a miraging haze caused by thermal inversion – and said that the iceberg appeared out of a haze. But, from their low vantage point, those in the lifeboats witnessed an incredibly clear night, while the crew of the *Californian* witnessed a false horizon that made *Titanic* appear much smaller than she was, so they thought they were looking at a ship that wasn't large enough to be fitted with radio equipment – perhaps a tramp steamer. They knew *Titanic* was in the area, they just didn't think the ship they could see was her.

Maltin also explains that the stratified layers of cold air near the sea 'effectively scrambled *Titanic* and *Californian*'s Morse lamp signals to each other', leaving crews unable to read each other's signals. Maltin also found reports of 'abnormal refraction' and 'mirage' in the logs of several ships that passed through the area before and after *Titanic* sank. He writes:

> Strong thermal inversions like this one are highly significant for navigation … [they allow] you to see much further than normal and [make] distant objects appear nearer than they really are … . At night the miraging on the horizon appears like a narrow bank of haze, due to light scattering in the very long air-path over the unusual distance you can see for and the trapping of light in a duct beneath the inversion.[7]

Despite these difficult miraging conditions, there *was* another way for the two ships to communicate. The *Californian* had a Marconi room manned by one Marconi Operator, Cyril Evans, but he was off shift when the *Titanic*'s Jack Phillips began sending CQD and SOS[8] Marconi messages in the desperate hope that nearby ships would pick them up. It was common practice in those days to employ just one Wireless Operator in a ship's Marconi room and to close the rooms between about 11 p.m. and 8 a.m. to allow the lone Operator time to eat and sleep; *Titanic* was unusual in having two Operators. But tragically for *Titanic*'s passengers and crew, the time Evans closed his Marconi room was just three minutes before *Titanic* collided with the iceberg.

Captain Stanley Lord's testimony to both the American and the British Inquiries is long and muddled[9] but, because of thermal inversion – although he didn't know it at the time – he assumed the lights he saw came from one small steamer signalling another.[10] He said, as did other witnesses who gave evidence to the Inquiries, that Cyril Evans was in touch with *Titanic*'s Marconi Operators *before* she collided with the iceberg and that one of them told him to 'Keep Out'. In his evidence to the American Inquiry, Evans said that was normal Wireless Operator language when there were many messages being transmitted. He said that, although it was possible to *hear* several messages from different ships at the same time, it wasn't possible for a Marconi Operator to *receive* or *send* a message clearly if other messages were coming in: those other messages caused interference. So if one of *Titanic*'s Marconi Operators was already receiving (or sending) a message to another ship's Operator, or to a land wireless station, when other messages were coming in, it was normal to say something like 'KO', meaning Keep Out, or 'Shut up'. It wasn't thought rude or wrong: it was the Wireless Operators' code.[11]

Jack Phillips, *Titanic*'s chief Marconi Operator, was busy sending messages on behalf of passengers before *Titanic* collided with the iceberg. In this extract from Captain Stanley Lord's evidence to the American Inquiry, held on Friday, 26 April 1912, just eleven days after *Titanic* sank, he talks about the *Californian*'s communications with *Titanic before* she collided with the iceberg:

> Senator SMITH. Did you attempt to communicate with the vessel *Titanic* on Sunday [14 April 1912]?
> Mr. LORD. Yes, sir.
> Senator SMITH. At what time of the day?
> Mr. LORD. Ten minutes to 11.
> Senator SMITH. a. m.?
> Mr. LORD. p. m ....
> Senator SMITH. What was that communication?
> Mr. LORD. We told them we were stopped and surrounded by ice.
> Senator SMITH. Did the *Titanic* acknowledge that message?

> Mr. LORD. Yes, sir; I believe he told the Operator he had read it, and told him to shut up, or stand by, or something; that he was busy.
> ...
> Senator SMITH. Did you have further communication with the *Titanic*?
> Mr. LORD. Not at all, sir.
> Senator SMITH. Did the *Titanic* have further communication with you?
> Mr. LORD. No, sir.[12]

There were other ships in the area but they were further from *Titanic* than the *Californian*. In Cyril Evans' evidence to the American Inquiry, he said he was sure *Titanic* had received his message about ice but he didn't expect a reply because he already knew her Wireless Operators were busy with other messages. If he'd included the code MSG with his message it would have forced a reply because MSG messages *have* to be sent to the bridge and acknowledged by a ship's Captain. Evans said:

> I was on watch until 5 and 20 minutes past 11. I heard the *Titanic* working. I put down the phones and I turned in.[13]

Titanic's Assistant Marconi Operator, Harold Bride, confirmed that he took the *Californian*'s ice message to Captain Smith. He remembers a slightly different message from Cyril Evans, but both confirm communication before *Titanic* collided with the iceberg:

> Mr. BRIDE. I received that message myself [from the *Californian* – although it was an earlier message, received at about 6.30 p.m.] and delivered it to the Captain. It stated that there were three large icebergs that the ship had just passed, and it gave their position.
> Senator SMITH. What was the hour of the day?
> Mr. BRIDE. Late in the afternoon, but I can not [sic] say the hour of the day.[14]

Lord said the message was sent at 'ten minutes to 11' at night, Bride that they received the *Californian*'s ice warning 'Late in the afternoon'. Either way there was no further communication between the two ships after *Titanic* collided with the iceberg because Cyril Evans had closed his Marconi room at 11.25 p.m. Dr Rudi Newman points out that *Titanic*'s clocks were twelve minutes ahead of the *Californian*'s – so it would have been 11.37 p.m. *Titanic* time, just three minutes before she collided with the iceberg.

In *A Night to Remember*, George Thomas Rowe, one of *Titanic*'s quartermasters, related that he obeyed Captain Edward Smith's orders to Morse signal 'that ship' and tell her, 'We are the *Titanic* sinking: please have all your boats ready.' Rowe signalled again and again but got no reply,[15] but his signals, as Tim Maltin's research has shown,[16] were scrambled by abnormal refraction, making them impossible to decipher.

When Harold Bride was preparing to change shifts with Jack Phillips, Phillips told him he thought *Titanic* had been damaged in some way. 'He expected we should have to go back to Harland & Wolff's [the Belfast shipyard].'[17] Phillips was about to go off shift when Captain Edward Smith came to their Marconi room. Bride told the American Inquiry his Captain said:

> Mr. BRIDE. 'You had better get assistance.' … Mr. Phillips … asked him if he wanted him to use a distress call. He said, 'Yes; at once.'
> Senator SMITH. Who sent this call?
> Mr. BRIDE. Mr. Phillips.
> …
> Senator SMITH. Was the message sent immediately?
> Mr. BRIDE. Immediately.
> Senator SMITH. Do you know what the message was?
> …
> Mr. BRIDE. CQD about half a dozen times; MGY half a dozen times … CQD is a recognized distress call; MGY is the code call of the *Titanic*.[18]

Bride never did change shifts with Phillips – he delivered messages to the Captain while Phillips stayed at the Marconi key. Guglielmo Marconi, who was at Harold Bride's hearing, confirmed that *Titanic* used the more modern SOS signal (from about 12.57 a.m. according to Dr Rudi Newman) as well as CQD. The *Frankfurt* was the first ship to pick up *Titanic*'s distress calls; Jack Phillips requested her position but got no reply. Then the *Carpathia* replied with her position. Harold Bride said:

> She [the *Carpathia*] sent her latitude and longitude and told him she was coming along as quickly as possible. She turned around and was steaming full speed, or words to that effect … [I took that message] to the Captain.[19]

Captain Smith returned with Bride to the Marconi room and asked what other ships Phillips had been in touch with. He said he was establishing communication with the *Olympic* and was waiting for the *Frankfurt* to reply. But *Titanic* never received any more replies. Twenty minutes after their original communication with the *Frankfurt*, her Marconi Operator, W. Zippel, had sent messages saying, 'What's the matter with you?' and 'What's up, Old Man?' He asked because by then *Titanic*'s power was failing and her CQD messages were no longer reaching the *Frankfurt*. Zippel had no idea why *Titanic* had fallen silent but the *Frankfurt* was hurrying towards *Titanic* by then, although Phillips didn't know it.[20] In the confusion – Phillips had been expecting Zippel to tell him they'd taken action as soon as he received his CQD call, not realising that the *Frankfurt*'s subsequent call had been a routine one and not a reply to his CQD – Phillips messaged back, according to Bride's evidence to the American Inquiry, that he was 'a fool' and 'to keep out of it' (out of communication) because, by then, he knew the *Carpathia* was their best bet for rescue. Afterwards, it was established that the *Frankfurt* was much further away from *Titanic* than Phillips originally thought (about 150 miles).[21] Harold Bride told the American Inquiry:

> Any Operator hearing a CQD giving a ship's position when on the job would immediately, without inquiring further into the matter, go to his Captain and inform his Captain. It would be a waste of time asking anything about it. The less time spent in talking, the more time can be spent in getting to the ship.[22]

Harold Cottam, *Carpathia*'s Wireless Operator, agreed with Harold Bride. He said, in his evidence to the American Inquiry, that any ship receiving Phillips' CQD calls should 'turn right around and steer for that position'.[23]

Because *Titanic* had two Wireless Operators, they worked in shifts, so her Marconi room operated twenty-four hours. And because there were two Operators they successfully managed, together, to mend their broken equipment the night before the disaster. Harold Bride said:

> Mr Phillips and myself had had a deal of trouble, owing to the leads from the secondary of the transformer having burnt through inside the casing and make [sic] contact with certain iron bolts holding the woodwork and frame together, thereby earthing the power to a great extent. After binding these leads with rubber tape, we once more had the apparatus in perfect working order, but not before we had put in nearly six hours' work, Mr. Phillips being of the opinion that, in the first place, it was the condensers which had broken, and these we had had out and examined before locating the damage in the transformer.
>
> Owing to this trouble, I had promised to relieve Mr. Phillips on the following night at midnight instead of the usual time, 2 o'clock, as he seemed very tired.[24]

Had *Titanic*'s Marconi Operators not managed to fix their equipment, it's possible no one would have been saved.

In his evidence to the American Inquiry, Captain Lord said they signalled with their Morse lamp often but, in Senator Smith's Report at the conclusion of the American Inquiry, he said:

> Had he [Captain Lord] been as vigilant in the movement of his vessel as he was active in displaying his own signal lamp, there is a very strong probability that every human life that was sacrificed through this disaster could have been saved.[25]

There's a much stronger possibility that more lives might have been saved if Captain Lord had woken Cyril Evans, his Marconi Operator, after James Gibson told him about the rockets. If Lord *had* woken Evans and asked him to find out if any nearby ships were sending distress signals, or any signal at all (even though he thought, because of abnormal refraction, caused by thermal inversion, that the signals he saw came from a vessel too small to have any radio equipment), those in Lifeboat Number 8 who were desperately

The *Californian*, commanded by Captain Stanley Lord, seen on 15 April 1912, from the *Carpathia*. Note the lifeboats are swung out, but the *Californian* didn't arrive until 8 a.m., five hours and forty minutes after *Titanic* sank.
(Image courtesy of Michael Pocock and Maritime Quest)

rowing towards the *Californian*'s lights wouldn't have had such a heartbreakingly futile struggle, and the ferrying process Captain Smith so confidently believed in might have happened.

Others argue that because *Titanic* sent out two signals with inaccurate positions that contradicted the positions of her rockets, and because the *Californian* would have had to find her way through an ice field to get to *Titanic*, she might not have arrived before the great ship began her final plunge. Even so, the *Californian would* have arrived and, if she had, it's possible that at least some of those struggling in the water would have been saved.[26]

Lord made a fatal mistake by not waking Evans.

And the *Californian*'s official logbook makes *no mention* of events during the Middle Watch (between midnight and 4 a.m.) on the morning of 15 April, the time when *Titanic*'s distress messages and signals were being sent repeatedly before she sank at 2.20 a.m.; the time when they were seen, even if distorted, by those in charge on board the *Californian*. Chief Officer Stewart, who wrote up the official log, told the British Inquiry that pages from the scrap log (the rough draft, from which an official log is verified and written up later) were destroyed on 'Company's instructions'. That company was the Leyland Line, owned by the International Mercantile Marine Company, which also owned the White Star Line. Third Officer Groves suspected the *Californian*'s scrap logbook might have been thrown overboard.[27]

Lord died in 1962 without ever successfully clearing his name. In his evidence to the American Inquiry, when describing the mistakes he and the *Californian*'s crew made when trying to distinguish lights from stars, he said:

> I pointed out to the officer that I thought I saw a light coming along, and it was a most peculiar light, and we had been making mistakes all along with the stars, thinking they were signals. We could not distinguish where the sky ended and where the water commenced. You understand, it was a flat calm [sea]. He [the officer] said he thought it was a star, and I did not say anything more.[28]

The 'most peculiar light' Lord saw was *Titanic*'s miraging masthead light, not her actual light. In *The Loss of the Titanic*, Lawrence Beesley wrote about one of *Titanic*'s distress rockets against the star-filled night:

> [It] leapt upwards to where the stars blinked and twinkled above us. Up it went, higher and higher … and then [there was] an explosion that seemed to split the silent night in two, and a shower of stars sank slowly down and went out one by one.[29]

Alfred Crawford said those in Lifeboat Number 8 didn't see any Morse signalling from the ship they were pulling for, even though they could see its masthead lights.[30]

As Thomas Jones and the only other sailor on board Lifeboat Number 8, Charles Pascoe, rowed their passengers away from *Titanic* across the icy water, pulling for the *Californian*'s lights in the vain hope of rescue, Jones heard Noël doing what she could to comfort the women on board, at least four of whom had had to leave their husbands behind. She reassured them that they – and all their beloved men – would find places in later lifeboats because she, like all *Titanic*'s passengers, had no idea there weren't enough. And because, as she said in her interview with *The New York Herald*, she knew 'something about boats', she would have reassured them in semi-nautical terms. She would have pointed out that the sea was calm so it was easier for those at the oars; that their lifeboat was sturdy and would keep them safe; that the clear night sky and bright stars made it possible for the able seamen to see the icebergs and to navigate.

Noël had the emotional capacity to comfort the women because she hadn't had to leave any menfolk behind, and later, either she volunteered to help Thomas Jones (see page 60) or he asked her what she knew about boats and she told him her husband kept a small racing yacht in Devonshire[31] so she knew how to take a tiller and she knew how to row. Either way, when they were safely in New York, Thomas Jones gave an account of the way Noël helped him in Lifeboat Number 8 to *The Daily Telegraph*, on 22 April 1912. He praised her 'determined' way during that long, frightening, freezing night. Here's a short extract (the full interview appears in Chapter Six):

> There was a woman on my boat as was a woman .... When I saw the way she was carrying herself ... I knew she was more of a man than any we had on board and I put her at the tiller.[32]

Gladys Cherry also took a turn at the tiller and both women took turns at the oars, as did other female passengers in Lifeboat Number 8. Noël said:

> A Mrs Smith [Swift] did yeoman service. She rowed for five hours with Tom Jones without taking a rest. Really, she was magnificent, not only in her attitude, but in the whole-souled way in which she worked. Mrs Pearson [Pears] also rowed, and my maid, Roberta Maioni, rowed the last half of the night.[33]

Alfred Crawford told both Inquiries that all four men, the two sailors, himself and a kitchen hand, 'took the oars and pulled away', and some women volunteered to help.[34] Crawford also confirmed Noël was at the tiller 'all night'.[35] Another passenger, Emma Eliza Bucknell, rowed beside Noël for part of the night, while her maid, Albina Bassani, rowed beside Noël's maid, Roberta Maioni, behind them.[36] Emma Bucknell also wrote:

> The plight of some of the women in our boat was pitiable. While some were fully dressed, others wore only their nightgowns and kimonos. The maid to the Countess Rothes, who pulled one of the best oars in the boat, was dressed in this fashion, and her hair was streaming down her back and shoulders all the time we were in the little boat. The women would row until they would fall from exhaustion, their place being

> taken by another woman who would gently move aside the collapsed one and work in her place until exhaustion also overcame her.
>
> Meanwhile, with our lamp burning low, we proceeded. We learned that one of the women on the boat [Mrs J. Stuart White] had an electric cane. She said the battery was in good shape, and she was delegated to flash it every once in a while.[37]

Marie Grice Young wrote that they:

> Depended on girls to steer us, and all night the women rowed, standing facing the men, so four hands were throwing all bodily strength into each pull of the oars.[38]

There was a lamp in the boat which, Alfred Crawford said:

> We lighted … and kept it burning. The wick kept falling down, but we kept raising it and lighting it. There was plenty of oil in the lamp.[39]

And all the boats 'had bread tanks. That I know for certain,' said Bruce Ismay to the American Inquiry. 'And they also had water breakers [barrels].'[40] Several survivors wrote afterwards that they couldn't find either water or food in their lifeboats,[41] but Marie Grice Young wrote that the Captain 'Threw a huge loaf of bread into the boat [Number 8]'.[42]

Fourteen of the lifeboats, including Lifeboat Number 8, had five pairs of oars; two smaller wooden lifeboats had three pairs; and the collapsibles had four pairs. The oars on all the boats were 'made of ash and tipped with leather-bound copper. They varied in length from fifteen to twelve feet.'[43]

Thomas Jones said, in answer to Senator Newlands' question about whether he could give him the names of any passengers on his boat:

> Mr. JONES. One lady. She had a lot to say, and I put her to steering my boat.
> Senator NEWLANDS. What was her name?
> Mr. JONES. Lady Rothe [sic]. She was a countess or something.[44]

In her sworn statement to the British Vice-Consul at Altadena, Noël said:

> After steering the boat for a short time, I changed places with a woman who was rowing and continued rowing for the rest of the night and Miss Cherry steered until we reached the *Carpathia*.[45]

Unsurprisingly, after a very traumatic night, accounts of who rowed when and who took the tiller when vary. But clearly Thomas Jones was impressed with the way Noël helped him, even though she didn't think she'd done anything particularly special. In *The Daily Graphic* on 30 April 1912, a first-class stewardess was reported telling Noël, '"You have made yourself famous by rowing in the boat" … . Lady Rothes replied, "I hope not; I have done nothing."' Obviously she was being modest: both she and Gladys Cherry did everything they could to help the commander of their lifeboat.

In Noël's letter to her parents she wrote:

> A little Spanish girl … was torn away from her husband just as I reached the top deck [the boat deck] – he put her into my arms, and asked me to take care of her. It was awful making her leave him, but one's only feeling was to prevent any panic or scene, & obey the Captain's orders – I had her in my arms most of part of the night. Her maid, a Spanish peasant, was quite incapable & useless – so terrified. Mercifully I managed to prevent her [the Spanish girl] seeing or hearing when the steamer sank as she was nearly mad … . [When she] began to scream for her husband it was too horrible. I left the tiller to

> my cousin and slipped down beside her to be of what comfort I could. Poor woman! Her sobs tore our hearts and her moans were unspeakable in their sadness …
>
> Gladys steered the boat nearly all night to let the men row – but it was too heavy & then four of us took turns … . The cold was intense & we were surrounded by icebergs that we expected would be on us any moment – for 2 hours we rowed hard towards a distant light, which was never any nearer.[46]

The 'little Spanish girl', Maria-Josefa de Satode Peñasco y Castellana, was the Prime Minister of Spain's niece and one of the younger survivors on board Lifeboat Number 8. She was 22; she was on her honeymoon and she'd had to leave her 24-year-old husband, Victor, behind. She never saw him again.

Noël said, in the Paris edition of her interview with *The New York Herald*, 'The goodbye was terrible.' And in her interview with the *Los Angeles Examiner* on 16 May 1912, she said:

> In this terrible blackness we rowed all night. Bits of ice bumped the sides of our craft. It was cold. Our hearts seemed chilled, but we hoped against hope that some one would pick us up.

If only Captain Stanley Lord had woken his Marconi Operator, Cyril Evans, when he saw that 'most peculiar light'. If he had, it's possible that the *Californian* would have been the 'some one' to pick up at least some of *Titanic*'s hapless passengers. If he had, it's possible that fewer female passengers would have become overnight widows, fewer children fatherless, fewer mothers childless and fewer men dead.

Six

Rescue

The horror of it all can never be told[1]

Lawrence Beesley survived in Lifeboat Number 13. He jumped into it from *Titanic*'s starboard side when no more women could be found and, like all the survivors, he spent a bitterly cold night in a small lifeboat. Lifeboat Number 8 was only half full, but Lifeboat Number 13 was packed so tightly that they stood in their boat (and Beesley said he would never think thirteen an unlucky number again). There were, Beesley wrote, sixty people on board, possibly more. His account of the disaster, *The Loss of the Titanic*, is lucid, straightforward and without drama.

Beesley's career as a science teacher might explain the clarity of his account (he also wanted to publish his book 'to see that the [Maritime Law] reforms so urgently needed are not allowed to be forgotten').[2] But I think he was also something of a poet because he wrote:

> The night was one of the most beautiful I have ever seen: the sky without a single cloud to mar the perfect brilliance of the stars, clustered so thickly together that in places there

> seemed almost more dazzling points of light set in the black sky than background of sky itself; and each star seemed, in the keen atmosphere, free from any haze, to have increased its brilliance tenfold and to twinkle and glitter with a staccato flash that made the sky seem nothing but a setting made for them in which to display their wonder. They seemed so near, and their light so much more intense than ever before, that fancy suggested they saw this beautiful ship in dire distress below and all their energies had awakened to flash messages across the black dome of the sky to each other; telling and warning of the calamity happening in the world beneath … . The complete absence of haze produced a phenomenon I had never seen before: where the sky met the sea the line was as clear and definite as the edge of a knife, so that the water and the air never merged gradually into each other and blended to a softened rounded horizon, but each element was so exclusively separate that where a star came low down in the sky near the clear-cut edge of the water-line, it still lost none of its brilliance. As the earth revolved and the water edge came up and covered partially the star, as it were, it simply cut the star in two, the upper half continuing to sparkle as long as it was not entirely hidden, and throwing a long beam of light along the sea to us.[3]

As Tim Maltin's research has shown, Beesley's description of the 'perfect brilliance of the stars', the 'complete absence of haze' and the stars losing none of their brilliance at the waterline was caused by thermal inversion, which in turn caused an abnormal refraction of light that made the night exceedingly clear to those in the lifeboats but distorted visibility for those on board the *Californian* and created a haze for those on *Titanic*'s bridge and in her crow's nest.

Maltin writes:

> Stars can never really be seen setting on the horizon … they always become extinct as they approach the real horizon, due

to the depth of air one is having to see them through at such a low altitude. What Beesley was actually seeing was the reflections of the stars on the distant sea surface, reflecting in the miraging duct at the horizon [caused by thermal inversion].[4]

In her interview with the *Los Angeles Examiner*, on 16 May 1912, Noël said, 'The night of the collision was the most beautiful of the trip.' But as she steered Lifeboat Number 8 while its commander, Able Seaman Thomas Jones, and others rowed, they heard screams and cries for help behind them as *Titanic* sank. The people who hadn't found a place in the far-too-few lifeboats were pitched into the icy water with only a few clothes and their lifebelts to protect them. Noël wrote to her parents:

> The horror of it all can never be told … those fearful cries when she sank will never go out of my head.[5]

As the passengers in Lifeboat Number 8 heard those 'fearful cries', an argument broke out about whether or not to go back to see if they could pick up at least some of the people struggling in the freezing water behind them. Thomas Jones put the idea to his passengers but the majority voted against. Marie Grice Young wrote that 'opinions were divided'.[6] In her interview with *The New York Herald*, Noël said:

> Tom Jones acted nobly, alternately cheering us with words of encouragement, then rowing doggedly … . The most awful part was seeing the rows of portholes vanishing one by one. We wished to turn back and rescue others, but the majority said 'No'.[7]

It must have been extremely difficult for Jones to obey his passengers: he was the lifeboat's commander, he could have ignored the majority and turned back to try to save more people. He wanted to with all his heart. Perhaps it was the rigid Edwardian class system that prevented him from going against their wishes: most of the women in his boat were first-class passengers, a very different social class from his own, in 1912. Or perhaps, knowing that his first duty was to his passengers, he reluctantly agreed not to turn Lifeboat Number 8 back when they reminded him at least once of his Captain's orders to 'row for the light'.

My great-grandmother wanted to turn back, so did Gladys Cherry and one other passenger, possibly Mrs Swift, possibly Dr Alice Farnham Leader. But I don't know what I would have done if I'd been there. I hope I would have had Noël's and Jones' courage and selflessness and joined them in wanting to turn back, but I know I would have been very frightened and I might have allowed my fear for my own life to get the better of my instinct to try to save others. The passengers in Lifeboat Number 8 were frightened of two things: first, if they turned back, when the desperate people in the water struggled to board their lifeboat it would turn over and twenty-seven more people would die. Second: as *Titanic* went down, there'd be a suction wave that would pull their lifeboat down with it and, again, twenty-seven more people would die.

Only one lifeboat did turn back: Lifeboat Number 14, commanded by another Welshman, Fifth Officer Lowe. His passengers confirmed his boat was the only one to do so.[8] The terrified majority of *Titanic*'s passengers and crew were left struggling in the water, behind the lifeboats, to die in the ice-laden water. They didn't drown but, perhaps mercifully quickly, they died from hypothermia.

Those who survived in the lifeboats faced the harsh reality of sitting in tiny boats on a vast ocean wearing life jackets, when they'd thought *Titanic* absolutely safe, a ship that *couldn't* sink, a ship whose owners had broadcast her inability to sink, a ship that should have taken them safely and comfortably to New York.

But it took the ship that had been designed to be unsinkable just two hours and forty minutes to sink: between 11.40 p.m. on Sunday, 14 April, and 2.20 a.m. on Monday, 15 April 1912.

In her letter to her parents Noël wrote:

> The endless hours in the dark on the water were the worst as one had time to think of everyone that we never expected to see again.[9]

But 3,000 miles away, on the other side of the Atlantic in Fife, Scotland, one of those people *was* thinking about Noël. Her eldest son, 10-year-old Malcolm, had woken up and told his nanny he knew his mother was cold and in danger. Much later, when Noël was safely home, Malcolm told her what had happened and they worked out that the time he woke, at around 4.45 a.m. GMT on Monday, 15 April, was the time she boarded Lifeboat Number 8; and the time he either wouldn't or couldn't go back to sleep before was seven hours later, at 11.45 a.m. GMT, the time Noël boarded the rescue ship, the *Carpathia*.

When the heartbreaking sounds of people dying in the freezing waters behind them stopped, the absolute silence broke the survivors' hearts. In an attempt to distract those in Lifeboat Number 8 and to cheer them at least a little, to keep up their flagging spirits, Gladys Cherry and/or Mrs Swift suggested they sing. And sing they did. They sang every ballad, every nursery rhyme, every folk song, every hymn … any song they could think of. And when they ran out they began again.

In his interview with *The Daily Telegraph* on 22 April 1912, Thomas Jones reported the singing. Here's the full text of that interview, which begins:

> The Countess of Rothes is now at the Ritz-Carlton Hotel, New York under the care of a physician. [She was at the Plaza, but was interviewed at the Ritz-Carlton.] I learn it is not so much exposure and shock which have made her ill, as the effects of her hard labour in pulling at the oars. Her boat was likewise undermanned, because the crew preferred to stay behind.
>
> One able-bodied seaman, who shipped aboard the *Titanic* when she left Southampton, is tired and little listless and

> subdued from the things he lived through last Monday [15 April 1912]. But his eyes light up and his speech becomes animated when you ask him what part the women played in the trying hours after the *Titanic* sank.
>
> 'There was a woman in my boat as was a woman,' he told *The Daily Telegraph* representative yesterday. 'She was the Countess of Rothes. I was one of those who was ordered to man the boats, and my place was in No. 8 boat. There were thirty-five of us in that boat [now thought to be twenty-seven] mostly women, but some men along with them. I was in command, but I had to row, and I wanted someone at the tiller. When I saw the way she was carrying herself, and heard the quiet, determined way she spoke to the others, I knew she was more of a man than any we had on board, and I put her in command. I put her at the tiller, and she was at the tiller when the *Carpathia* came along five hours later.
>
> 'And there was another woman on board [perhaps Mrs Swift; perhaps Gladys Cherry] who was strong in the work we had to do. She was at the oar with me, and though I never learned her name she was helping every minute. It was she who suggested we should sing. "Sing? you say!" I should think we did! It kept up our spirits. We sang as we rowed, all of us, starting out with, "Pull for the Shore," and we were still singing when we saw the lights of the *Carpathia*. Then we stopped singing and prayed.'[10]

And at last, after just under seven[11] long, bitterly cold hours among the icebergs in the ice field, the frightened, freezing lifeboat passengers saw what Lawrence Beesley described as 'a faint far-away gleam in the southeast'. Until they saw that gleam, *Titanic*'s survivors had no idea if anyone else knew what had happened, if anyone else would ever come to their rescue. They didn't know if they'd survive.

Beesley wrote:

> We all turned quickly to look and there it was … streaming up from behind the horizon like a distant flash of a warship's searchlight; then a faint boom like guns afar off, and the light died away again … . And then, creeping over the edge of the sea where the flash had been, we saw a single light, and presently a second below it, and in a few minutes they were well above the horizon … . We did not know what sort of a vessel was coming, but we knew she was coming quickly, and we searched for paper, rags, – anything that would burn (we were quite prepared to burn our coats if necessary).[12]

Noël wrote, in her letter to her parents:

> It was not until 5 or 5.30 that we caught sight of the steamer – & at first could not believe she could be really there & that we might be rescued.[13]

And, in her interview with the *Los Angeles Examiner* on 16 May 1912:

> Up over the horizon came a black vapor. Eyes turned upon this beacon and hearts beat faster. It was smoke: it meant rescue. I cannot describe the feeling that came over me as I saw the masts, then the deck houses, and finally the hull of the *Carpathia* as she raced toward us.[14]

Thomas Jones, who was rowing beside Noël at that point, turned to her and whispered (see pages 86 and 87).

It took Lifeboat Number 8 at least another hour to reach the rescue ship but, once they'd seen her, they and all the passengers in all the other lifeboats knew for certain that someone was coming to help them. Imagine their relief.

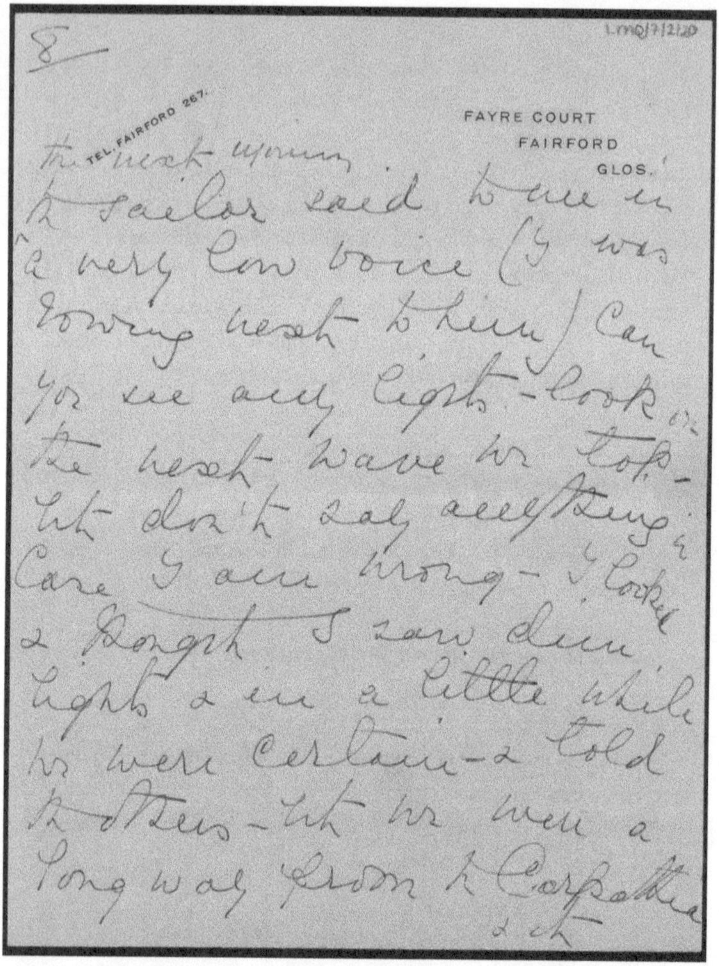

8

LMQ/7/2/20

TEL. FAIRFORD 267.

FAYRE COURT
FAIRFORD
GLOS.

the next morning the sailor said to me in a very low voice (I was rowing next to him) Can you see any lights – look on the next wave we top – but don't say anything in case I am wrong – I looked & thought I saw dim lights & in a little while we were certain – & told the others – but we were a long way from the Carpathia & it

Page 8 of Noël Rothes' twenty-page 1955 letter to Walter Lord, for his book *A Night to Remember*. Noël beautifully recaptures the hope she and Jones felt on first seeing the *Carpathia*. (Image courtesy of the National Maritime Museum, Caird Library, reference LMQ/7/2/20)

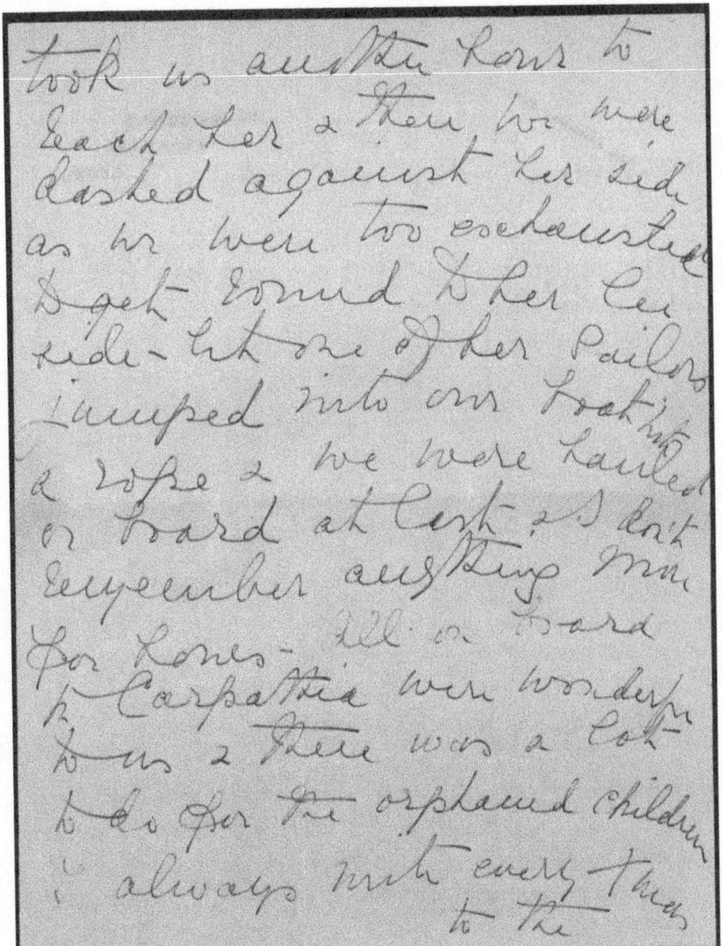

took us another hour to
reach her & then we were
dashed against her side
as we were too exhausted
to get round to her lee
side – but one of her sailors
jumped into our boat with
a rope & we were hauled
on board at last & I don't
remember anything more
for hours – All on board
the Carpathia were wonderful
to us & there was a lot
to do for the orphaned children
I always write every Xmas
to the

Page 8, reverse, of Noël Rothes' twenty-page 1955 letter to Walter Lord, for his book *A Night to Remember*. Boarding *Carpathia* was difficult, but 'all on board … were wonderful … . I always write every Xmas to the [sailor T-Jones].' (Image courtesy of the National Maritime Museum, Caird Library, reference LMQ/7/2/20)

Marie Grice Young wrote:

> Our hearts surged to the belief that help, relief and life itself reached out glad, welcoming hands … . As far as eye [sic] could see, were small white boats struggling towards the rescuers called by the miracle of the wireless message.[15]

The *Carpathia* was bound from New York to Gibraltar and was some 58 miles away when Captain Arthur Rostron read *Titanic*'s distress message, brought to him by Harold Cottam, his Marconi Operator. In his 1931 book, *Home from the Sea*, Rostron wrote about how he questioned Cottam and how he made decisions about what to do next:

> 'Are you sure it is the *Titanic* that requires immediate assistance?' I asked.
>
> 'Yes, sir.' …
>
> 'Tell him we are coming along as fast as we can.' …
>
> I at once worked out the course and issued orders. Within a few minutes of the call we were steaming all we knew to the rescue. The *Carpathia* was a fourteen-knot ship, but that night for three-and-a-half hours she worked up to seventeen knots … There was much to be done. All hands were called, and then began over three hours of restless activity and never-ending anxiety … Racing through the dark towards we knew not what danger from bergs, standing on the bridge with every one [sic] keeping a bright look out, I was fully conscious of the danger my own ship and passengers were sharing.
>
> I may say now [1931] that the spring of that year [1912] was phenomenal in regard to ice. The *Titanic* was on her right course, a course where … one at times may see ice, but that night was so exceptional as to be unique in anyone's memory. The reason was that two summers before the season had been unusually warm in the far north. Islands of ice had broken adrift from their polar continent and come drifting south. It

> took two years for these giant remnants to work their way so far south and we were to be amazed when daylight broke to find on every hand berg and floe stretching as far as the eye could reach …
>
> We were ploughing on through the night – a brilliant night of stars … The sense of tragedy was growing … The *Titanic* had … asked how long we should be getting up. 'Say about four hours,' I told the Operator [Cottam] (we did it in three and a half hours), 'And tell her we shall have all our boats in readiness and all other preparations necessary to receive the rescued … company's rockets to be fired from 3 a.m. every quarter of an hour to reassure the *Titanic*'.[16]

Thomas Jones said he'd only ever seen one iceberg in the six years he'd served on the *Majestic*, another White Star Liner that worked the Atlantic crossing.[17] Captain Rostron, who'd sailed the north Atlantic track for many years, told the British Inquiry, 'I never remember seeing ice in April on the track.'[18]

When Noël arrived on the deck of the *Carpathia*, she – like so many other survivors – was utterly exhausted. She wrote:

> I fainted when I was being taken on board which was stupid but I think it was the strain of the last hours' rowing & the cold – so I remember nothing after I was put into the swing & hauled up until I found myself on the dining room sofa with the Doctor pouring hot stuff down my throat – & someone rubbing me.[19]

The heartbreaking tragedy of the night of 14–15 April 1912 is that, of the 2,208 passengers and crew on board – people who'd sailed confidently believing in *Titanic*'s safety; people who so keenly anticipated their arrival in New York – only 712 souls were saved. Three died in the lifeboats, and one more died aboard *Carpathia*; one of those four might have been Jack Phillips, whose body was never recovered. Harold Bride confirmed his colleague's death and burial at sea, but he never actually saw Phillips alive or dead after they left *Titanic* – he was simply told he was aboard the same lifeboat.

When Senator Smith asked Bride which lifeboat he was saved in he said:

> There were no big lifeboats on the ship [by then] … . There was a collapsible boat on the top deck at the side of the forward funnel [on the port side] … . It was pushed over on to the boat deck … and went over the side … I went over with it.[20]

The boat was upside down and Bride was under it, but eventually the boat was righted and he climbed into it. He joined 'a big crowd'. By then he'd spent some time in the freezing water and his feet suffered. When Bride was asked if Jack Phillips died going from the *Titanic* to the *Carpathia*, he said:

> Mr. BRIDE. He died on the way; yes. He died on board the upturned boat.
> Senator SMITH. What became of his body?
> Mr. BRIDE. As far as I know, it was taken on board the *Carpathia* and buried from the *Carpathia*.
> Senator SMITH. Buried at sea?
> Mr. BRIDE. Buried from the *Carpathia*.[21]

But it seems this didn't happen.

George Behe writes, in his article 'The Fate of Jack Phillips', that neither Harold Bride nor Charles Lightoller actually saw Phillips or his body. (Lightoller, *Titanic*'s Second Officer, was on board the same collapsible lifeboat and said Jack Phillips was too.) It's also possible, according to a steward who survived in the same lifeboat, Thomas Whiteley, that Phillips died in a different lifeboat. Behe concludes:

> Sadly, this is probably as close to solving the mystery of Jack Phillips' death as we will ever come.[22]

In *Home from the Sea*, Captain Rostron wrote that the *Carpathia* 'Picked up seven hundred and six persons'.

We know now that 712 is the number of those who were saved, although it still remains possible that many more people might have been saved that night if the White Star Line management, including Bruce Ismay and Harland & Wolff's designers, hadn't so faithfully trusted that *Titanic* was designed and built to be a practically unsinkable 'lifeboat in itself' – a ship that, if she did eventually sink, would remain afloat long enough to ferry all her passengers and crew to safe ships, exactly as happened when the White Star Line's *Republic* sank in 1909.

Heartbreakingly, *Titanic*'s lifeboats and their commanders never had the opportunity to do that.

Captain Arthur Rostron, Captain of the *Carpathia*, who, within a few minutes of receiving *Titanic*'s Marconi CQD message from Jack Phillips, steamed 'all we knew to the rescue' and 'picked up 706 persons'. (Image courtesy of George Grantham Bain Collection, Prints & Photographs Division, Library of Congress, LC-USZ62-121011. Words from *Home From the Sea*, 1931)

Seven

On Board *Carpathia*

They got the message four minutes before their Marconi place closed for the night[1]

Harold Cottam, *Carpathia*'s Marconi Operator, reported receiving the first of *Titanic*'s distress messages at approximately 11.30 p.m., but he said that was a 'rough estimate', because he didn't make a procès-verbal (a written report).[2] *Titanic* collided with the iceberg at 11.40 p.m. but *Carpathia* actually picked up her first distress message at 12.37 a.m. *Titanic* time (*Carpathia* was about seventeen minutes ahead of *Titanic* time, so about 12.54 a.m. her time).[3]

Here's Cottam's evidence to the British Inquiry:

> SOLICITOR-GENERAL (John Simon[4] – who also represented the Board of Trade): Now tell us, as nearly as you can, it is only a recollection, I understand – what it was which the *Titanic* said to you?
>
> HAROLD COTTAM: She said, 'Come at once; we have struck a berg,' and sent his position, and then he sent CQD … I asked him if he intended me to go straight away to the bridge and get the ship turned round immediately, and he said, 'Yes, quick.' …

SOLICITOR-GENERAL: And did you tell her that you were coming to her assistance?
HAROLD COTTAM: I did .... He said: 'Come as quickly as possible, old man, the engine room is filling up to the boilers.' ...
SOLICITOR-GENERAL: Did communications continue between you and the *Titanic*?
HAROLD COTTAM: That was the last I heard of the *Titanic*, that message. At 11.55 [p.m. – probably New York time; 1.57 a.m. *Titanic* time].[5]

Noël found the time to write her letter to her parents on 18 April 1912, three days after *Titanic*'s survivors were winched to safety aboard *Carpathia*. In this extract she writes about the few saved men, about arriving at *Carpathia*'s side, about her fellow survivors and those on board the rescue ship:

> Very few 1st class men were saved unless we hear news of more survivors at New York. There are 15 widows alone in the 1st class ... The sea was very calm till day-break & then began to get up a little, & by the time we managed to row to this steamer it was rather rough for small boats & we dashed repeatedly against the side of this ship & were then hauled up on a little plank & rope.
>
> You cannot imagine the goodness of all these people [the crew and passengers on board *Carpathia* who did what they could for *Titanic*'s survivors, including giving up their cabins] – they came at full speed to the rescue, all among the icebergs – & at great risk to themselves, over 60 miles under 3 hours. The Captain told me they got the message 4 minutes before their Marconi place was closed for the night.[6]

Just four minutes.

Arthur Rostron told the American Inquiry:

> The whole thing was absolutely providential .... The Wireless Operator [Cottam] was in his cabin at the time, not on official

business at all but just simply listening as he was undressing. He was unlacing his boots [Cottam said, in his witness evidence, he'd taken his coat off] .... He had [the] apparatus on his ear, and the message came .... In ten minutes, maybe he would have been in bed, and we would not have heard the messages.[7]

If Harold Cottam hadn't been awake with his wireless apparatus still on his head, if he'd already closed his Marconi room, *Titanic*'s exhausted and freezing lifeboat passengers wouldn't have been picked up until almost three hours later, when the *Californian* arrived, at 8 a.m. But 8 a.m. was five hours and forty minutes after *Titanic* sank, far too late for the majority of her passengers and crew who'd been thrown into the freezing water when she sank at 2.20 a.m.

At the American Inquiry, Senator Smith asked Guglielmo Marconi why Marconi rooms were almost always single-manned and not kept open for twenty-four hours:

Senator SMITH. If this Operator is not at his post of duty, has the wireless message no signal to arouse him?
Mr. MARCONI. Not the way it is installed on most boats ....
Senator SMITH. Ought it not be incumbent upon ships at sea who have the wireless apparatus to have an Operator always at his key?
Mr. MARCONI. I think it certainly should be. Of course, it might come rather hard on small ships. The shipowners will not like the expense of two men.[8]

It was usual for a single Marconi Operator's cabin to double as his wireless room, but *Titanic*'s Marconi room had a separate sleeping cabin. Harold Bride reported to the American Inquiry that Jack Phillips sent *Titanic*'s distress signals at the request of the Captain. Bride was off shift and asleep in their shared cabin when the collision happened. When Phillips received *Carpathia*'s reply to his CQD, which read, 'Fifty-eight miles away and coming hard',[9] he sent Bride up to the wheelhouse to give Captain Smith the message, but although Phillips had confirmation that help was on its way, he died before it arrived. He never heard the rockets *Carpathia* fired, never saw her lights and never saw *Titanic*'s survivors being taken on board, but his CQD message had summoned the rescue ship – even if too late for him and so very many others. As he died, perhaps in the well of one of the lifeboats that others were rescued from (see page 90), I hope he knew that as many souls as possible would be saved by his CQD message to *Carpathia*. I hope he comforted himself by telling himself he'd done his duty. I hope he believed he wasn't dying in vain.

There's a memorial to him in his birthplace, Godalming, in Surrey.

However, for the majority of *Titanic*'s passengers and crew, even *Carpathia* wasn't quick enough. Despite the speed she made, she arrived at 4 a.m., an hour and forty minutes after *Titanic* sank, too late to save anyone who hadn't been lucky enough to find a place in a lifeboat. Her Captain, Arthur Rostron, said he stopped his engines at four o'clock when he was close to the first boat.[10] In his evidence to the American Inquiry, he said:

> At 8 o'clock [a.m.] the Leyland Line steamer *Californian* hove up, and we exchanged messages. I gave them the notes by semaphore about the *Titanic* going down, and that I had got all the passengers from the boats .... He then asked me if he should search around [to see if there were any more boats, or bodies] and I said, 'Yes, please.' It was then 10:50 [a.m.] ... At 8:30 all the people were on board.[11]

Cyril Evans, the *Californian*'s Marconi Operator, told the American Inquiry he was woken by his Chief Officer, Mr Stewart, at about 3.30 a.m. on Monday, 15 April (an hour and ten minutes after *Titanic* sank). The Officer told him a ship had been sending up distress rockets in the night. (At another point in his evidence Evans said it was a ship's mate who woke him.) But by the time Evans was woken, the terrible total of 1,496 of *Titanic*'s passengers and crew were already dead.

Evans didn't know why he hadn't been woken before. He said, in his evidence to the American Inquiry:

> Senator SMITH. [Mr Stewart wanted] … you [to] see if there was anything the matter?
> Mr. EVANS. Yes, sir.
> Senator SMITH. What did you do?
> Mr. EVANS. I jumped out of bed … and I went at once to my key and started my motor and gave 'CQ' About a second later I was answered by the *Frankfurt* 'DKD, Dft.' The 'Dft,' is the *Frankfurt*'s call. He told me the *Titanic* had sunk … .
> Senator SMITH. Do you know why you were not called when the rockets were first seen?
> Mr. EVANS. No, sir.[12]

The *Frankfurt* changed course and steamed towards *Titanic* as soon as its Marconi Operator, W. Zippel, realised she was in serious trouble, but they were too far away to arrive before she sank. Zippel told Evans early that morning that they were '30 or 40 miles off. We are steaming as fast as we can' towards *Titanic*'s last communicated position.[13]

There's a document included in the *Titanic Inquiry Project*[14] that lists the reported positions of ships and their distance from *Titanic* when her distress calls were being sent out. It confirms the *Californian* was by far the closest ship and was the ship whose lights Noël said that they 'rowed hard towards … but which was never any nearer'.[15]

The complete text of Noël's letter to her parents follows (extracts appear elsewhere in this book). It was written on board *Carpathia* on 18 April 1912, three days after *Titanic* sank. The punctuation is copied from the original, which is now lost. *Carpathia* arrived in New York on the evening of 18 April, at 9.30 p.m., but they hadn't expected to arrive until early on 19 April.

My darling Mother,
This letter of course is for Father too, but I cannot write you much yet – + can never never tell you all the horrors we have been through since Sunday – of course, we had no men belonging to us thank God – for the people who had, it has been too ghastly –

I am afraid you will have been in great anxiety, if you heard the news, before the names were published – I sent you a Marconi as soon as I could –

We struck the iceberg at ¼ to 12 on Sunday night, at first, and until nearly one o'clock, no one realised any danger – or really knew what had happened – then the order came to be dressed + have lifebelts on, in ten minutes – + we were then put into the life boats at ¼ to 2. – she sank with over 1,200 people before our eyes.

The boats were none of them very full and very few 1st class men were saved unless we hear news of more survivors at New York – there are 15 widows alone in the 1st class – one or two piteous – a little Spanish girl [Maria-Josefa de Satode Peñasco y Castellana] who was torn away from her husband just as I reached the top deck – he put her into my arms, and asked me to take care of her – it was awful making her leave him, but one's only feeling was to prevent any panic or scene, + obey the Captain's orders – I had her in my arms most of part of the night – her maid, a Spanish peasant, was quite incapable + useless – so terrified – Mercifully I managed to prevent her seeing or hearing when the steamer sank as she was nearly mad. – the other English + American women in our boat with one exception were splendid + we had 24 of them – 1 seaman, + only 2 stewards, who did not even know how to row. – Gladys steered the boat nearly all night to let the man [sic] row – but it was too heavy + then four of us took turns – one American woman rowed without stopping for five hours – The cold was intense + we were surrounded by icebergs, that we expected would be on us any moment – for 2 hours we rowed hard towards a distant light, which was never any nearer – Some of us wanted to return to the ship to try + pick up people but the majority were against this, + said we should be sucked in by the sinking ship so we had to give it up –

We got into the boat a little before 1.30 – + it was not until 5 or 5.30 that we caught sight of the steamer – + at first could not believe she could be really there + that we might be rescued.

The sea was very calm till day-break + then began to get up a little, + by the time we managed to row to this steamer [Carpathia] it was rather rough for small boats + we dashed repeatedly against the side of this ship + were then hauled up on a little plank + rope –

You cannot imagine the goodness of all these people – they came at full speed to the rescue, all among the icebergs – + at great risk to themselves, over 60 miles under 3 hours – The Captain told me they got the message 4 minutes before their Marconi place was closed for the night – + he then had all the crew up + told them that he left it to them to do their best that night –

We are over 700 on board + of course have nothing with us but the clothes we managed to put on – some of us very little –

Maioni [Noël's maid] was in our boat + behaved splendidly – I sent her up at once when the order came, but she wanted to wait for us, which I of course did not allow – but it was grand at a moment like that – I just had time to pour out some brandy, give her some, + Gladys + myself + hurriedly dress – then no-one seemed to know where the lifebelts were kept, + a strange man found ours for us – we then tied on his for him – + all shook hands + told each other that it would not be long before we met again – as we all thought there were plenty of boats – little knowing that there were *only 16 – + that there were 3,000 people on board – [there were 20 lifeboats and 2,208 people on board].*

It was like a terrible nightmare – + endless – but for the people who had husbands – of course 2 or 3 wives stayed with them – it seems too cruel to separate people unless there are children. Gladys and I are all right though of course very tired. I fainted when I was being taken on board which was stupid but I think it was the strain of the last hours' rowing + the cold – so I remember nothing after I was put into the swing + hauled up until I found myself on the dining room sofa with the Doctor pouring hot stuff down my throat – + someone rubbing me –

Then a poor Hungarian woman went quite mad, thinking her tiny baby was missing – but it was found –

There is plenty to do now helping the Doctor with the tiny children – feeding them + letting the Mothers rest – I find my French very useful, there are so many who know no English – this morning the Doctor sent for me to be with a French woman who was quite frantic – + we were afraid to leave her – it took 2 hours to calm her as she declared she would kill herself – but is quiet now – but must not be left –

The little Spanish lady is quite dazed now – but clings to me like a baby – she knows no one at all in America except one man in Washington.

– The 2nd + 3rd class are easier to quiet + manage + are so grateful for any little gift or attention – one steerage woman has lost 7 children out of 8 and her husband – but oh the horror of it all can never be told + those fearful cries when she sank will never go out of my head – and I am one of the lucky ones –

We are in a fog now so I am afraid we shall be late in New York + we so long to arrive – most of the people are so splendid, tho' a few have broken down –

Gladys has been busy distributing the garments we can collect + make, to the children – we have made great friends of course with some of the people + one marvels at their heroism – tho' one did not really feel frightened + mercifully there were so many to help + see to; the endless hours in the dark on the water were the worst as one had time to think of everyone that we never expected to see again –

I have written you much more than I thought at first I could + it's rather a relief tho' one can never explain many details till we meet –

I hope Mother got my Marconi soon [sic] – I will of course write again from New York. We must be there a little while to get things, we are hoping against hope for more news of survivors tomorrow – but the Captain told me privately he had none – so one says nothing. The Dr. here is so kind + helpful to us both.

Fondest love,
Noël[16]

In *Home from the Sea*, Arthur Rostron wrote about the service they held on board *Carpathia* for all those who died, and how they gave thanks for those who'd been saved. He wrote that his crew comforted the rescued, persuaded them to eat and did their best to 'soften the grief which wrapped them round about'. He wrote about the way his doctors looked after *Titanic*'s survivors and gave them their own clothes, and how the male passengers gave up their cabins and many of the women doubled up to leave their cabins free for *Titanic*'s survivors. He wrote that his officers also gave up their cabins and how in his own cabin, which he gave up, there were:

> Three ladies, each of whom were bereaved. Their husbands, all millionaires, had perished and, in addition, one lady had lost a son.[17]

Titanic survivors on board the *Carpathia*. Ian Leslie, 21st Earl of Rothes, Noël Rothes' grandson, thought the woman sitting sewing, in the middle of the picture, was his grandmother. (Chronicle/Alamy Stock Photo)

Noël said, in her interview with the *Los Angeles Examiner* on 16 May 1912, that everyone on board the rescue ship was extremely kind and did everything they could for *Titanic*'s survivors. But even their kindness 'could not bring back lives'.

When, in her letter to her parents, she wrote that she was 'one of the lucky ones', of course she meant she was lucky to survive but most of all she meant she hadn't had to suffer what so many female passengers suffered as they boarded the lifeboats: the overwhelming grief of leaving behind a man they loved – a husband, a father, a brother, an uncle, a cousin, an adult son, a fiancé, a friend. My great-grandmother never had to say the final heart-wrenching farewells those women had to say to their menfolk, never had to imagine them going down with the ship, alone and frightened. But by the time those women were safely aboard *Carpathia*, they knew without doubt that they were never going to see their beloved menfolk again.

In *On Board RMS Titanic: Memories of the Maiden Voyage*, George Behe quotes Elizabeth Shute, a first-class survivor:

> Lifeboats kept coming in, and heart-rending was the sight as widow after widow was brought aboard. Each hoped some lifeboat ahead of hers might have brought her husband safely to this waiting vessel. But always no.[18]

Here's Gladys Cherry's second letter to her mother, dated 18 April 1912, written on board *Carpathia*. She talks about those widowed women, among other things. (In all Gladys' letters reproduced here, the punctuation and spelling are copied from the originals: she was writing only days after very traumatic experiences.)

> I think we all feel a little better this morning, we, that are so fortunate, having lost no one; but all the poor womens [sic] faces are piteous to see; yesterday morning I was very busy with a Ships [sic] Bosun, cutting out garments for the Steerage and Second Class children, some of whom had no clothes at all, we made little coats and leggings out of the blankets. Then I went round the Steerage and Hospitals with the Doctor, who is a charming man, and he said a cheery face and word did so much for them, our *Titanic* men most of them with legs and feet frozen are wonderful when you think what they have been through … We are Supposed to get to New York tonight, but we are still in fog; under ordinary circumstances they would not land us at night, but perhaps now they will, if you could only imagine how we long for land – This water all around is terrible, and ones [sic] nerves now seem worse than on that dreadful night.
>
> The Doctor gave me a little Bromide last night and I slept a little better, but one wakens terrified, which is very silly, as we have nothing to grumble at in comparison with the poor widows, Oh it is too dreadful to see them, Nöel [sic] and I have helped in seeing after these poor distressed souls, and it has helped us so much … .

One girl has just come up and given me a pair of stockings and gloves to land in, as my stockings were all ripped up that night in the boat, people are so good – one lady who has her husband (only about five of them have), is an American and she is going to ask a friend of hers to take us round in her car in New York in the morning to buy some things, as we have nothing but what we stand up in, we could have taken so much in our pockets if we had realised, but the only thing I took up was the little photograph of you, then I though [sic] 'how silly' we shall soon be back here and I put it down again; it is all such a horrible nightmare, one don't [sic] think of it at all and the nights are so awful.

I dread the voyage back again, I am afraid this fog will prevent us getting in tonight, and I can't stand another night on the sea; all the crew, Captain passengers and stewards are perfectly sweet to us; there are two little French children 3 years and 20 months old, who have lost their father and I take one of them every day for a bit while the mother rests. [I think these are Joseph and Juliette Laroche's children. Lester J. Mitcham's lists in the appendices to the book *Report into the Loss of the SS Titanic*, between pages 285 and 311, identify children.][19]

I love to do something, it stops one thinking. I hope we shan't have another accident in this fog – Noels [sic] poor maid [Roberta Maioni] is very sick, she was sick all the way from Cherbourg but she behaved splendidly in the boat that night.[20]

For everything Noël did to help *Titanic*'s survivors, for the help she gave Able Seaman Thomas Jones in Lifeboat Number 8 and for the work she did on board *Carpathia*, sewing blankets into coats and doing her best to comfort the survivors, the crew nicknamed her 'the Plucky Little Countess'. The name stuck and several newspapers quoted it.

On 4 May 1912, the *Fifeshire Advertiser*, a newspaper local to Leslie House, the Rothes' family seat in Fife at the time, published a poem about her. The article's title was 'A Plucky Little Countess'. It reads:

The conduct of the Countess of Rothes is greatly praised in the press. A stewardess said all the women spoke with admiration of Lady Rothes, who rowed all night in her boat and devoted herself during the whole time she was on the *Carpathia* to the care of the steerage women and children. She helped to make clothes for the babies, and became known as 'The plucky little Countess'.

The following verses, which appeared in a recent issue of 'The Standard' newspaper, will be read with interest : –

THE LITTLE LADY
By JOHN SAVILE JUDD[21]
(It will be remembered that the Countess of Rothes, who is an expert oarswoman, took charge of one of the lifeboats of the *Titanic*. The entire management of the boat fell to her, none of the men in it having any expert knowledge of seamanship or of the art of rowing.)

Press exaggeration about *Titanic* annoyed my great-grandmother very much: Able Seaman Thomas Jones was a seasoned sailor and there was a second able seaman on board Lifeboat Number 8, Charles Pascoe. The poem below also exaggerates: Noël wasn't at the tiller all night and it was either Gladys Cherry or Mrs Swift who suggested they sing. There's no record of what Noël thought about the poem, but she was a modest woman: when it was suggested she'd made herself famous by rowing in her lifeboat (see page 76) she said she'd done nothing, so she probably wasn't particularly impressed by it. But she did keep the press cutting and it is a tribute to her steadfastness that night. The cutting – a version without a newspaper attribution – appears in my mother's first album near the beginning. The poem printed below comes straight after the introductory words in the *Fifeshire Advertiser* above.

It is rather more a jingle than a rhyme;
The metre may be wrong,

For the meaning of the song
Is somehow much more precious than the time,
Being all about the lady
At the tiller of the boat –
The boat the little lady
Kept afloat.

All aboard the boat were fearful – of the cold:
Their voices seemed so weak
When they did their best to speak
That, soon, they only did as they were told
By the clear-voiced little lady
At the tiller of the boat –
The boat the gentle lady
Kept afloat.

The women had to pull the boat in turn:
The cold was felt no more
As each struggled with an oar,
And all that could not row were made to learn
By the quiet little lady
At the tiller of the boat –
The boat the noble lady
Kept afloat.

She worked a living miracle on board:
She tempted them to sing,
Just a snatch of anything,
Till they lifted up their hearts unto the Lord,
With the gallant little lady
At the tiller of the boat –
The boat the loyal lady
Kept afloat.

Any time at all will do to shout
in honour of her name:
For her light is a steady flame,
And many could not bear to do without
The splendid little lady,
The good angel of the boat:
Through her, who knows how many
Kept afloat?[22]

This postcard of sand sculptures was found among Noël Rothes' *Titanic* papers in 1956, when she died. The sculpture on the right is an image of her as the 'Plucky Little Countess'. (Image courtesy of Claes-Göran Wetterholm)

Thomas William Jones, in his early forties, *c.*1920. Underneath his coat is the fobwatch Noël gave him, to thank him for everything he did in Lifeboat Number 8 on the night *Titanic* sank. (Trinity Mirror/Mirrorpix/Alamy Stock Photo)

A poster advertising *Titanic*'s maiden voyage. (G.P. Essex/Alamy Stock Photo)

These Scottish freshwater pearls were the only jewellery Noël Rothes wore when she left *Titanic*: the rest went down with the ship. Her husband gave them to her for their wedding. (Image courtesy of the Leslie family)

Malcolm Leslie, Noël Rothes' eldest son *c.*1912–14. In 1927, he became the 20th Earl of Rothes. But on the night *Titanic* sank, 15 April 1912, when he was 10, he woke up knowing his mother was cold and in danger. (Unknown artist. Image courtesy of the Leslie family)

Thomas Dyer-Edwardes, Noël Rothes' father, disembarked *Titanic* at Cherbourg. If he hadn't, he almost certainly would have died when the men were asked to stand back. (Copy of a painting by John Collier [d.1934]. Image courtesy of Joanna Hitchcock, granddaughter of May Goodman, Noël Rothes' first cousin)

Clementina Georgina Lucy Dyer-Edwardes, Noël Rothes' mother. Her birth name was Drummond-Villiers. She also disembarked *Titanic* at Cherbourg. (Copy of a painting by John Collier [d.1934]. Image courtesy of Joanna Hitchcock)

The roundel Thomas Jones made for Noël Rothes. He sent it to her with a letter dated 29 September 1912, asking her to accept it, 'in respect for your courage under so terrifying circumstances'. (Image © David Brown)

The inside of the fobwatch case that Noël Rothes gave Thomas Jones to thank him for everything he did in Lifeboat Number 8. It shows the inscription: 'April 15th 1912, from the Countess of Rothes'. (Image © David Brown)

The clock face of the fobwatch. (Image © David Brown)

The back of the fobwatch case. I wonder if the initials might be a C and a J entwined, for Countess and for Jones? (Image © David Brown)

A sapphire and diamond ring given to Noël Rothes by Maria-Josefa's father, for looking after his daughter in Lifeboat Number 8 and afterwards. Maria-Josefa was on her honeymoon; she was 22. Her 24-year-old husband, Victor, went down with the ship. (Image courtesy of the Leslie family)

Wreck of the RNLI lifeboat *Lady Rothes*. Before her sad wrecking, she served the Fraserburgh community for twenty-two years (1915–37) and saved sixty-five lives, the number that *could* have been saved in Lifeboat Number 8. (Image © James Gray, Gray & Adams, Fraserburgh)

Wreck of *Titanic*'s bow on the seabed. (Courtesy of NOAA/Institute for Exploration/University of Rhode Island)

Plaque in memory of Twm (Tom) Titanic, as he's known where he was born, at 4 Sea View, Cemaes Bay, north Anglesey. The plaque was unveiled in 2023. (Author)

Memorial to Thomas Jones and Noël Rothes in Cemaes Bay, north Anglesey. It stands below the house where Jones was born, facing out to sea. *Titanic* is printed on its prow. Maker: Steve Blackwell of Blackwell's Stonecraft. Unveiled, 2022. (Image © Gareth Jones – no relation)

Noël Rothes' husband, Norman Evelyn Leslie, 19th Earl of Rothes, in 1904, in the uniform of the Royal Company of Archers (the King's Bodyguard for Scotland). He was 27 and known as Evelyn, but formally Rothes. (Painting by George Percy Jacomb-Hood (d.1929). Image courtesy of the Leslie family)

Lucy Noël Martha Leslie, Countess of Rothes (birth name Dyer-Edwardes and, from December 1927, Mrs Claud Macfie, although she kept her title), but always known as Noël. The photograph was taken on 26 April 1917, when she was aged 38, perhaps for her wedding anniversary on 19 April. (© Bassano Ltd. Courtesy of the National Portrait Gallery)

Eight

Letters and Gifts

I would rather drown with them than leave them[1]

A little while after *Titanic*'s survivors were all safely on board *Carpathia*, thirteen of her lifeboats were winched aboard. The rest were set adrift.[2]

In *Home from the Sea*, Arthur Rostron wrote:

> We got as many of the *Titanic*'s boats as we could on board, some remaining suspended in our davits, others hauled on the forecastle head, and proceeded.[3]

And sometime between when the lifeboats had been winched aboard and the evening of 18 April 1912 when the *Carpathia* arrived in New York, Thomas Jones went in search of Lifeboat Number 8, and when he found her he prised the two bronze 8s from either side of the prow and put them in his pocket. They were, approximately, 4in long. It's possible he took the 8s from his boat after the lifeboats were moored in New York Harbor – people did take things from *Titanic*'s lifeboats – but I think it's much more likely he took them while on board *Carpathia*, because when he arrived in New York he was quickly escorted, with all the crew, to the *Lapland*.

Either way, several months after the disaster Noël Rothes received a wooden roundel in the post, made for her by Jones: the bronze 8 from his lifeboat was set at its heart, Noël's name and his name were hand-printed in gold lettering above the 8 and the name of the ship and the date she sank were hand-printed below.

Before Jones sent Noël the roundel, she sent him a fobwatch she'd had engraved for him to thank him for the work he did so 'nobly' for all his passengers in Lifeboat Number 8. The engraving was simple, it read: 'April 15th 1912', and below it, 'from The Countess of Rothes'. The fobwatch is no longer in the Jones family – it was sold – but Noël's grandson, Ian Rothes, bought it back at auction in 1999. There was also a postcard from Jones to his fiancée, Miss L.C. (Clara) Moulton, with the fobwatch that shows a tram in The Avenue, Southampton. Jones wrote that he'd been to collect a parcel and discovered a watch and chain from Noël.

Noël also gave Alfred Crawford an engraved fobwatch. They didn't keep in touch, but her present suggests he took an oar and pulled away, as he told both Inquiries (see page 74) despite disparaging remarks about the men in Lifeboat Number 8 published before the poem about Noël (see pages 105–107), and even in Noël's and Gladys' own letters to their mothers. Crawford's fobwatch was bought fraudulently for £15 from its unwitting owner by a jeweller in 1999. But there was a court case, the jeweller was found guilty and fined and the fobwatch was returned. Although, later, it too was put up for auction.[4]

After Jones received his fobwatch from Noël, he wrote her a thank you letter and, in the years after the disaster, they wrote to each other. They always wrote at Christmas, when Noël would enclose £1 with her letter. Jones' granddaughter, Shelagh Oakes, told me her mother used to say that that £1 'did Christmas'. It paid for everything. (£1 in the early twentieth century would be worth about £400 in terms of purchasing power in 2025.)

Jones' first letter to Noël was sent from the Southampton Sailors' Home, where he stayed for some time after the disaster; it is dated 28 June 1912. The original of this letter is in the first of my mother's albums, towards the end.

He wrote:

> My Lady,
> I have only today received your very gracious present [the fobwatch], and I appreciate, very much, the honor extended to me by Your Grace in acknowledging any service rendered by me at the time of the disaster – which was my duty to those of whom I was in charge.
> May I say how much service you rendered myself and others by your example and courage under so heartrending circumstances.
> I shall always treasure your kind gift as my priceless possession.
> I have the honor to be,
> Your Grace's Obedient Servant,
> T Jones[5]

When Jones sent Noël the roundel he sent a letter with it, dated 29 September 1912, also from the Southampton Sailors' Home. The original of this letter is also in my mother's first album.

> My Lady,
> I beg to ask your acceptance of the number of my boat from which you were taken on board S/S *Carpathia*.
> This number is the original taken from the boat by myself. In asking you to accept the same, I do so in respect for your courage under so terrifying circumstances.
> Trusting you are now fully recovered to health,
> I am, your obedient servant,
> Tom Jones A.B., late S/S '*Titanic*'[6]

Noël treasured her roundel as much as Jones treasured his fob-watch. When she wrote to thank him for it, she said, 'I cannot tell you how much I appreciate it and I shall always value it as one of the greatest of my possessions.' That letter was auctioned

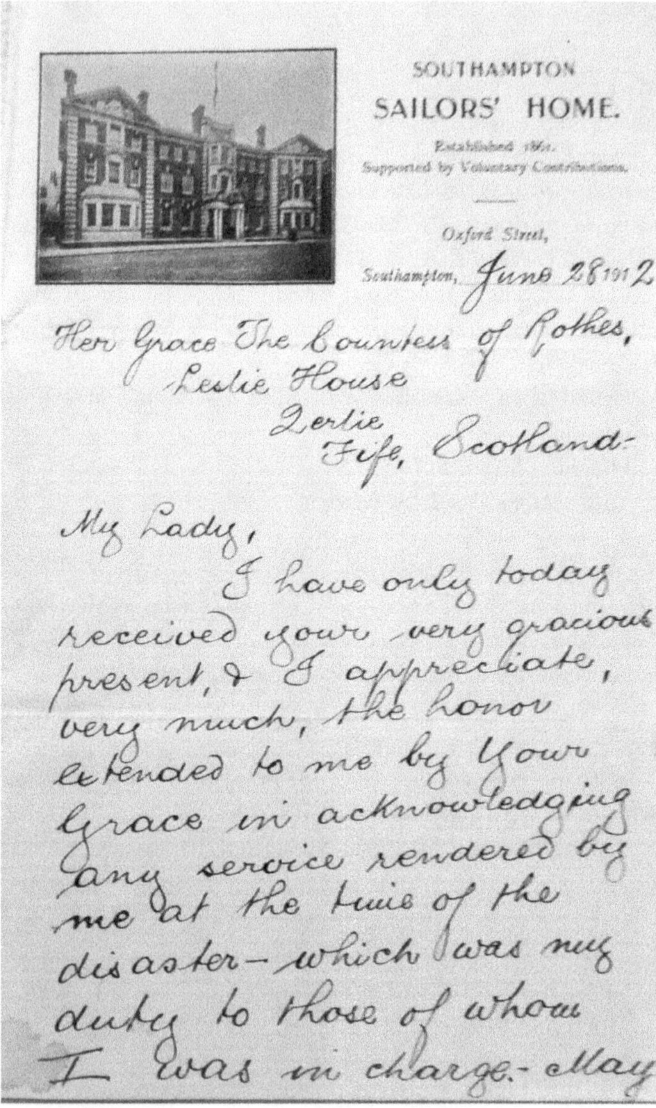

SOUTHAMPTON
SAILORS' HOME.
Established [illegible].
Supported by Voluntary Contributions.

Oxford Street,
Southampton, June 28 1912

Her Grace The Countess of Rothes,
Leslie House
Leslie
Fife, Scotland.

My Lady,
I have only today received your very gracious present, & I appreciate, very much, the honor extended to me by Your Grace in acknowledging any service rendered by me at the time of the disaster – which was my duty to those of whom I was in charge. – May

Thomas Jones' first letter to Noël Rothes, 28 June 1912, thanking her for the fobwatch.

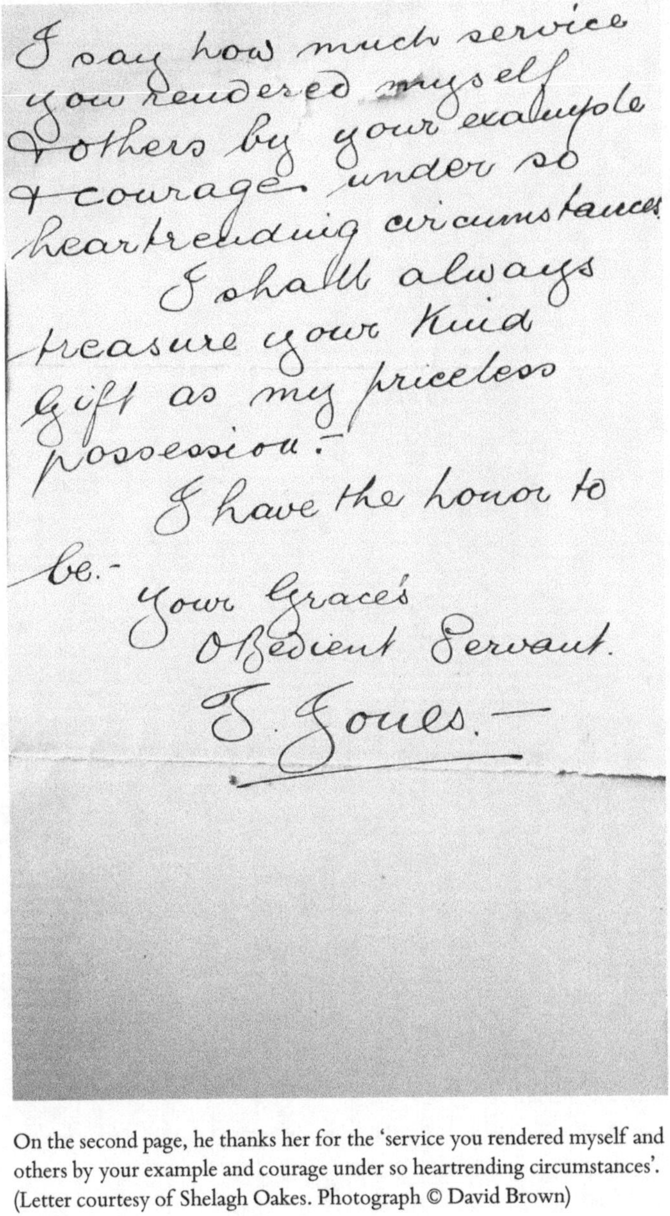

I say how much service
you rendered myself
& others by your example
& courage under so
heartrending circumstances.
I shall always
treasure your kind
gift as my priceless
possession.
I have the honor to
be.-
Your Grace's
Obedient Servant.
T. Jones.—

On the second page, he thanks her for the 'service you rendered myself and others by your example and courage under so heartrending circumstances'. (Letter courtesy of Shelagh Oakes. Photograph © David Brown)

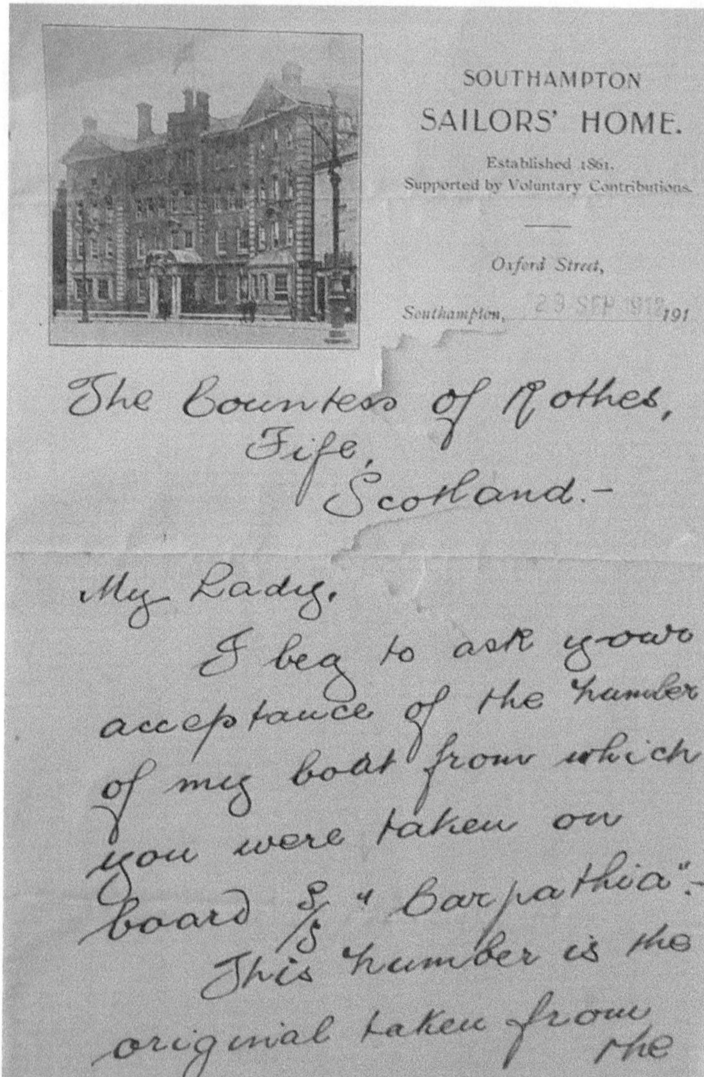

SOUTHAMPTON
SAILORS' HOME.
Established 1861.
Supported by Voluntary Contributions.

Oxford Street,
Southampton, 29 SEP 1912 191

The Countess of Rothes,
Fife,
Scotland.-

My Lady,
I beg to ask your acceptance of the number of my boat from which you were taken on board S/S "Carpathia".-
This number is the original taken from the

Thomas Jones' second letter to Noël Rothes, 29 September 1912, asking her to accept the roundel he'd made for her.

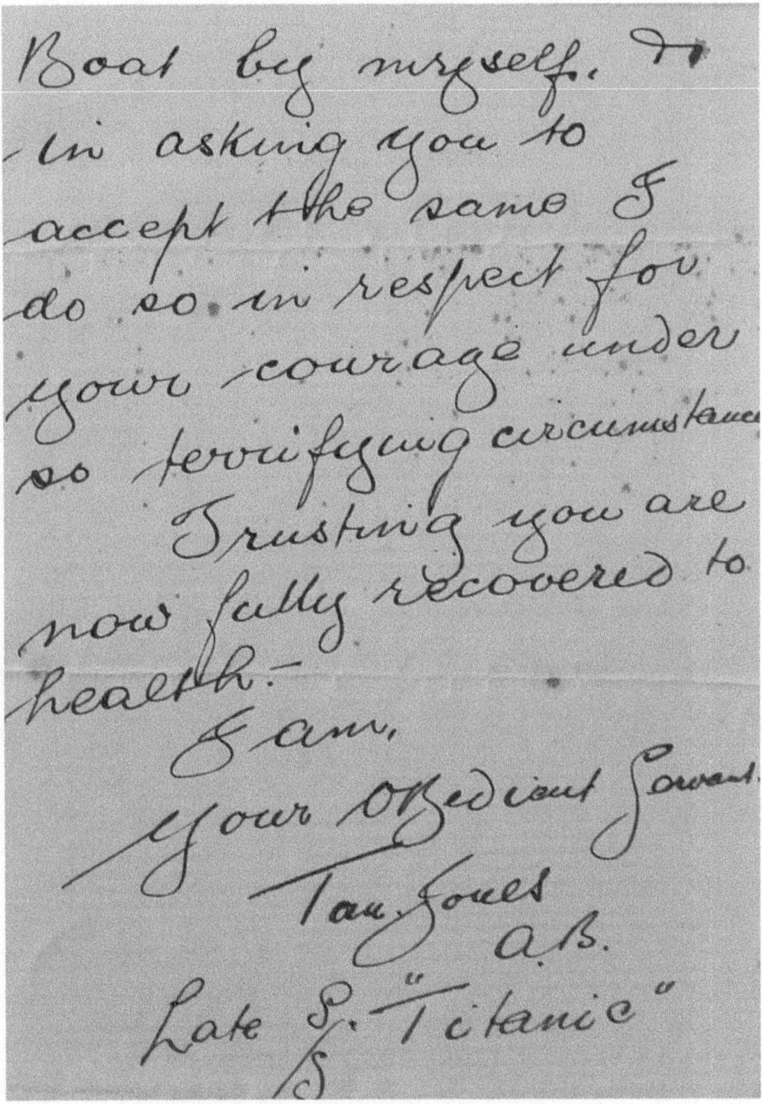
Boat by myself. &
in asking you to
accept the same I
do so in respect for
your courage under
so terrifying circumstances
Trusting you are
now fully recovered to
health:-
I am,
Your Obedient Servant.
Tom Jones
A.B.
Late S. "Titanic"
S

The second page says that the roundel he'd made was 'in respect for your courage under so terrifying circumstances'. (Letter courtesy of Shelagh Oakes. Photograph © David Brown)

with the fobwatch when Jones' family sold it (when Ian Rothes bought the fobwatch back he didn't buy the letter, but I've seen the Auction House outline transcript) and Noël did treasure the roundel her whole life; it clearly held great emotional value for her, and Jones' words about her 'courage under so heartrending circumstances' and her 'courage under so terrifying circumstances' bring home how frightening the night in the lifeboat was and how they both did everything they could in entirely unexpected and very difficult circumstances. Although Jones recorded that all he did was his duty and Noël said, when praised for what she'd done, that she'd done nothing.

In 2012, the hundredth anniversary of the disaster, Nell Jones, Thomas Jones' youngest daughter, and I met when the BBC made a short documentary about our ancestors.[7] Nell told me she remembered the letters her father wrote to Noël and the replies he received, because he used to read them to her. But when she told her school friends her father was writing to a countess they didn't believe her. She told me, with a smile, that as a girl she thought 'everybody knew a countess'.

Gladys Cherry also wanted Jones, and as many people as possible, to know how 'wonderful' he'd been when he commanded Lifeboat Number 8. She wrote to him to say so, but to make sure his courage and competence reached as wide an audience as possible, she sent her letter to *The Morning Post*, from where it was syndicated to national and international newspapers. Those press cuttings were found in Noël's box of *Titanic* papers and now they're in my mother's first album.

Gladys wanted Jones, and the wider world, to know that he'd done everything he could on that terrible night; that he'd been a truly splendid commander of Lifeboat Number 8. *The Morning Post* printed her letter on 27 May 1912. The title above it was 'Praise for a Welsh Sailor'. Here it is, published in the *Wells Journal* on 30 May 1912:

Lady's Praise of a *Titanic* Seaman

> One of the able seamen on the *Titanic*, Thomas Jones, a native of Anglesey has received the following letter from New York: – [Gladys wrote from the Northern Hotel]
>
> I feel I must write and tell you how splendidly you took charge of our boat on the fatal night. There were only four English [British] people in it – my cousin (Lady Rothes), her maid, you, and myself, and I think you were wonderful.
>
> The dreadful regret I shall always have, and I know you share with me, is that we ought to have gone back to see whom we could pick up, but, if you remember, there was only an American lady [possibly Mrs Swift, possibly Dr Alice Farnham Leader], my cousin, self, and you who wanted to return.
>
> I could not hear the discussion very clearly as I was at the tiller, but everyone forward, and the three men, refused.
>
> But I shall always remember your words … .

The words Gladys Cherry always remembered were the ones Thomas Jones said when the majority on board Lifeboat Number 8 refused to turn back to see if they could help any of the desperate people struggling in the freezing water behind them.

He said, as Gladys Cherry recorded:

> Ladies, if any of us are saved, remember I wanted to go back. I would rather drown with them than leave them.

Gladys ended her letter with:

> You did all you could and – being my own countryman – I wanted to tell you this. Yours very truly, Gladys Cherry.[8]

The *Wells Journal* article continued:

> It seems that Jones was in charge of a boat in which there were 35 ladies and three men. Capt. Smith ordered him to row for a light which they saw in the distance, put the passengers in safety, and return to the *Titanic* as soon as possible. He failed to reach the light, and when he saw that the *Titanic* had sunk he wanted to go back and save some of those struggling in the water, but was overruled. After eight hours in the open boat they were picked up by the *Carpathia*.[9]

Perhaps the icy water would have claimed the lives of those struggling behind Lifeboat Number 8 before they reached them, had they turned back. Perhaps not. There are differing reports about how many more people Fifth Officer Lowe managed to save in Lifeboat Number 14: some say four more were rescued and two died; some that three more were rescued and one died.[10] But it is possible that Thomas Jones could have rescued several more in his lifeboat; the fact that he didn't turn back haunted him.

Sometime after receiving the roundel from Jones, Noël received a sapphire and diamond ring, a gift from Maria-Josefa de Satode Peñasco y Castellana's father. Noël looked after Maria-Josefa in Lifeboat Number 8, on board *Carpathia* and in New York until she could take safe passage home to Spain. Some say sapphires are symbols of protection and good fortune; some, of kindness and wise judgement. I have no way of knowing whether Maria-Josefa's father knew the symbolism of sapphires, but he must have felt Noël possessed those qualities as she looked after his 22-year-old, newly widowed daughter.

Maria-Josefa and Noël kept in touch for forty-four years after the disaster; one of the letters found in Noël's box of *Titanic* papers was from her. Jean Mackenzie, my aunt, said it was dated 2 September 1956, just ten days before Noël died. Sadly the letters between Noël and Maria-Josefa are lost, but the sapphire and diamond ring, now a clasp for a pearl necklace, is still in the family.

Thomas Jones' noble conduct – as Noël described it – saved twenty-seven people in Lifeboat Number 8. But clearly he wanted to turn back to do what he could to save more because he knew his lifeboat could hold sixty-five people. If he had turned back, it's possible he might have saved another thirty-eight people and, if not that many, at least a good few more. My heart breaks for him when I think about his willingness to drown with them rather than leave them.

Nine

What Went Wrong and What Changed Afterwards

Laws relating to the preservation of life are not adequate[1]

The things my great-grandmother and Thomas Jones witnessed the night *Titanic* sank prompted me to ask questions about why so few people survived. I really wanted to understand what happened and why. What follows is a catalogue of the things that went wrong and what might have been done to prevent at least some of the deaths.

There Weren't Enough Lifeboats

In her letter to her parents, Noël Rothes wrote: 'We all thought there were plenty of boats.' *Titanic*'s passengers had no reason to think there weren't enough lifeboats but there weren't, for the reasons shown in Chapter Three. *Titanic*'s lifeboat capacity was 1,178,[2] but there were 2,208 people on board. It would have been difficult to launch the extra boats that were once planned (see pages 37–38) because *Titanic* sank so quickly. But what if the lifeboat loading had begun as soon as possible, as a precaution? And what if *Titanic had* carried those extra lifeboats? A good few hundred more people might have been saved.

A Lifeboat in Itself

If the White Star Line hadn't believed *Titanic* to be 'a lifeboat in itself', if the idea of her 'unsinkability' hadn't embedded itself among her passengers and crew, more lifeboats would have left with as many people as they could carry. If that had happened, perhaps 500 more lives might have been saved. And if *Titanic*'s designers had *imagined* the damage an iceberg might cause, perhaps her hull would have been stronger and able to defend her against it.

Eight (of Twenty) Lifeboats Left *Titanic* with Fewer than Fifty People on Board

According to the British Inquiry's lifeboat figures,[3] five of the port lifeboats and three of the starboard lifeboats left with fewer than fifty people on board: one had as few as seventeen, another twenty-six. (A new study details who was in which lifeboat.)[4]

Fourteen of the lifeboats could have taken sixty-five people each (910); two could have taken forty each (80); and the four Englehardt collapsibles, forty-seven each (188), making a total lifeboat capacity of 1,178. It's true that the early lifeboats left without their full quota of passengers partly because people didn't want to board them, preferring to stay on the safe, unsinkable (as they thought) ship. Also, Second Officer Lightoller stuck strictly to women and children first and Captain Smith believed a ferrying process between *Titanic* and another ship would happen. Two of the collapsibles proved impossible to launch upright by the end, but they did act as rafts until the people clinging to them were transferred to other boats.[5]

But with minor overloading of five extra people in each of the sixty-five-person lifeboats, between 480 and 560 more lives might have been saved,[6] and if the extra lifeboats *had* been carried – lifeboats planned to future-proof the Olympic Class liners against a likely change in Maritime Law but never installed on *Titanic* (see pages 37–38) – a further 800 people might have been saved. It's important to note that these lifeboat capacities are for boats crammed with people standing up, so when fully loaded like that, there might have been difficulties when the sea became rougher in the morning. And in a lifeboat filled to capacity there would have been limited room for the sweep of the oars.[7] But even so … if the lifeboats had left with more people on board, another few hundred souls might have been saved.

In a hypothetical case where the extra sixteen lifeboats *were* carried (see pages 37–38) and *all* lifeboats left *Titanic* slightly overloaded, 1,300 of the remaining 1,496 souls might have been saved (500 + 800 = 1,300). It would have been very difficult, perhaps impossible, to get all those lifeboats away in the short time between *Titanic*'s collision with the iceberg and the time she sank (two hours and forty minutes) but might the boats have been cut loose as she was sinking? Could people have clambered on board from the freezing sea as some did on to the collapsible lifeboats? I wonder.

No Help from the *Californian*, the Nearest Ship

Thomas Jones gave evidence to the American Inquiry that he 'pulled for the light', but found he could not get 'near the light'. That light came from the *Californian* but thermal inversion caused abnormal refraction, which made Morse signal identification very difficult. But if Captain Stanley Lord had woken his Marconi Operator, Cyril Evans, to find out if there were any radio signals coming in, things might have been very different. He didn't wake Evans because the atmospheric conditions made *Titanic* look too small to carry radio equipment. Even so he should have, to make sure. If he had, Jack Phillips' CQD and SOS Marconi messages would have been picked up by the *Californian*.

Report into the Loss of the SS Titanic states that the *Californian*'s Third Officer Groves suspected her scrap logbook had been thrown overboard. A damning suspicion. But the book also states that even if Lord had taken immediate action only 100 more lives might have been saved.[8] But that's still a possible 100 lives.

Ships Not Required to Keep Marconi Rooms Open Twenty-Four Hours

Unusually, *Titanic* had two Marconi Operators; the *Californian* and the *Carpathia* only had one each. Cyril Evans, of the *Californian*, closed his Marconi room at 11.37 p.m. *Titanic* time, just three minutes before she collided with the iceberg at 11.40 p.m. If the law had required Marconi rooms to be manned twenty-four hours, or if they had had signal-detecting alarms to wake a single Operator, the *Californian* would have picked up *Titanic*'s CQD messages. The Marconi equipment was fledgling technology, so these rules weren't yet established. But what if Cyril Evans had still been awake, as Harold Cottam had been on board *Carpathia*?

No Safety Drill

There wasn't a safety drill at sea and even though, in 1912, such drills were only for the crew, because there wasn't one, the crew weren't adequately prepared for a total evacuation on this, *Titanic*'s maiden voyage. If there had been a drill, the crew would have known which lifeboats were assigned to them and they'd have been better acquainted with the new Welin davits from which the boats were lowered. It's possible that fewer lifeboats would have left half or less than half full and 500 more lives could have been saved.

In a *New York Herald* article on 20 April 1912, it was suggested there should be a drill for passengers as well, despite the fact that:

> Steamship companies do not wish to [remind] the passengers of anything so unpleasant as … an emergency in which they would have to take to the boats.

It would have been good if they had.

Among the press cuttings found with Noël's *Titanic* papers was this one, from 20 April 1912:

> To the Editor of *The Morning Post*
> REAL CREWS FOR LIFEBOATS
>
> Sir: - May I suggest (1) that there should be sufficient accommodation in the lifeboats for all on board; (2) that each lifeboat should have its own appointed men, ready at once to take command in case of the boats being required; and (3) that every man joining the ship in any capacity should be certified as being able to row, as there are not many heroines like the Countess of Rothes. Yours, &c, INA DURRANT Scottow Hall Norwich

Bulkheads Too Low

Titanic's watertight bulkheads were overwhelmed. Of her fifteen, eight reached D Deck and seven reached E Deck, but they proved too low when the iceberg scraped along her starboard hull. If they'd reached beyond D Deck, *Titanic* would have remained afloat for longer and there'd have been more time for rescue ships to arrive. Mark Chirnside points out that the fundamental reason *Titanic* sank was that too many watertight compartments were flooded, not that her bulkheads failed to act as they were designed to act. But, in 1913, a year after *Titanic* sank, the *Olympic*, her sister ship, had her watertight bulkheads extended up to B Deck.[9] Which speaks for itself, I think.

Low Gates to Third Class

Lawrence Beesley noticed the gates between third class and other decks were low; John E. Hart said the barriers could be lifted out by hand, but a steward (or a quartermaster) usually stood by them to prevent third-class passengers from exploring the rest of the ship. As a result, third-class passengers had never been to the boat deck and when ordered up to it they didn't know their way and/or had difficulty understanding what they were being asked to do: approximately half the third-class passengers weren't native English speakers.

In *Report into the Loss of the SS Titanic* this account appears (also on page 39):

> There is too much circumstantial evidence (passenger accounts, existing gates on her two sister ships etc.,) for us to conclude that *Titanic* had no physical barriers that prevented at least some third class passengers from reaching the boat deck.[10]

Had there been notices in several languages with directions about how to get around the ship, and had the stewards been ordered to call third-class passengers up sooner, fewer lifeboats would have left half or less than half full, saving a few hundred more lives.

No Statutory Ice Patrol

If there'd been statutory ice patrols in 1912 and a law that set a speed limit in difficult or dangerous conditions, (a) *Titanic* would have been officially warned about the ice, and (b) the officer on watch would, by law, have had to slow *Titanic*'s speed in the ice field. *Titanic* was travelling at the 'standard procedure' speed, but had she been travelling at a slower speed she might have been able to avoid the iceberg altogether.

Only One Lifeboat with Spare Capacity Turned Back

Lifeboat Number 14 turned back, under the command of Fifth Officer Lowe. But it was the only one; more lifeboats should have turned back. Thomas Jones desperately wanted to turn his lifeboat back despite the risks and the refusal of the majority of his passengers. More souls could have been saved if he – and others – had turned back.

Maritime Law Failed to Keep Pace with Contemporary Technological and Shipbuilding Advances

In 1912 Maritime Law was governed by the Merchant Shipping Act, 1894. It was eighteen years out of date. That law set a tonnage of 10,000 as the calculation point for the number of lifeboats a liner should carry, but by 1912, much larger liners were being built. *Titanic* was 46,328 tons. Even though larger ships didn't always carry more passengers than their smaller counterparts, if *Titanic*'s *actual* tonnage had been used as the calculation point for the number of lifeboats she should carry, she would have carried four times the number and there would have been a lifeboat place for every single soul on board.

But in 1912 lifeboat calculations were based on the fact that ships were thought to be lifeboats in themselves and 'practically unsinkable'. Lifeboats weren't thought of as life savers but as ferries. Their purpose was to ferry passengers and crew between ships in the unlikely event of an 'unsinkable' ship sinking. And even then, the thinking at the time was that a ship's watertight equipment was designed so a ship would sink slowly (the *Republic* took nine hours to sink in 1909, see page 31).

There are so many 'if onlies'. If only:

– There'd been enough lifeboats;
– 'Boats for all' had been fitted on *Titanic* as Cunard decided to fit on *Aquitania* in February 1912, before her launch in 1914;

– Contemporary faith in shipbuilding technology hadn't convinced *Titanic*'s owners she couldn't sink;
– Her owners and designers had *imagined* the damage an iceberg might cause and so designed *Titanic*'s hull so that she might resist it;
– Captain Stanley Lord had awoken his Marconi Operator;
– All Marconi rooms had been double-manned and kept open twenty-four hours;
– There'd been a crew safety drill *and* one for the passengers;
– The bulkheads had been higher;
– Third-class passengers had been called up to the boat deck sooner and some of them hadn't been prevented from reaching it at all;
– There'd been permanent ice patrols and a law limiting speed in ice fields or avoiding them altogether;
– More lifeboats had turned back;
– Maritime Law had kept pace with shipbuilding technology.

All these things were addressed by lawmakers relatively soon after *Titanic* sank (see pages 132–133). But the true tragedy for all those who died is that adequate laws for the safety of life at sea didn't exist in 1912. If they had, many, many more people, if not all, might have lived.

Men died in far greater numbers than women and children and, of those men, passengers and crew died in almost equal numbers. The numbers of third-class male passengers who died outnumbered those in both first and second class (although, as a proportion of those who set sail, 92 per cent of second-class men died while 86 per cent of third-class men died, but only 167 second-class men set sail while 452 third-class men set sail).[11] The deaths of third-class women and children outnumbered those in first and second class. Three female crew died.

It remains a heartrending fact that just over twice the number of those who lived, died: 712 lived; 1,496 died. In the appendices to the book *Report into the Loss of the SS Titanic* by the systems analyst and engineer Samuel Halpern and others, there's a fifty-one-page list of the names of all those who died and all those who lived, compiled by Lester J. Mitcham.[12] It stands as a memorial to them all.

On pages 129–130 there's an account in bare numbers, which appears in Halpern's book, on page 67:

Passengers								
	Men		Women		Children		Total	
First Class	176		143		5		324	
Second Class	167		95		22		284	
Third Class	452		181		76		709	
Total Number of Passengers	795		419		103		1,317	
	Lost	Saved	Lost	Saved	Lost	Saved	Lost	Saved
First Class	118 (67%)	58 (3%)	4	139 (20%)	1	4	123	201
Second Class	154 (92%)	13 (13%)	12	83	0	22	166	118
Third Class	392 (86%)	60 (50%)	90	91 (61%)	46	30	528	181
Number Lost/Saved	664	131	106	313	47	56	817	500

Tables to show, separately, the numbers of passengers and the numbers of crew (following page) – divided into men, women and children – who died or survived, from George Behe, Samuel Halpern et al., *Report into the Loss of the SS Titanic*, page 67. (Courtesy of Samuel Halpern)

Crew						
	Men		Women		Total	
Deck Department	66		---		66	
Engine Department	325		---		325	
Victualling Department	477		23		500	
Total Number of Crew	868		23		891	
	Lost	Saved	Lost	Saved	Lost	Saved
Deck Department	23	43	---	---	23	43
Engine Department	253	72	---	---	253	72
Victualling Department	400	77	3	20	403	97
Number Lost/Saved	676	192	3	20	679	212

In his concluding speech to the American Inquiry, Senator Isidor Rayner recommended changes to:

> The admiralty and navigation laws of this country. They consist of an incongruous collection of antiquated statutes which should be repealed and reenacted so as to meet the necessities of ocean intercourse of the present day. This is surely one lesson that has been taught us by this dreadful calamity.[13]

The British Inquiry concluded with twenty-four recommendations for change, including to watertight compartments, lifeboat provision, safety drills and more.[14]

Both the American and the British Inquiries concluded that *Titanic* should have slowed down once she'd been warned of ice in the area by other ships. The American Inquiry criticised the British Board of Trade. An article on *Britannica* online sums up the American Inquiry's conclusion:

> The US investigation faulted the British Board of Trade, 'To whose laxity of regulation and hasty inspection the world is largely indebted for this awful fatality'. Other

contributing causes were also noted, including the failure of Captain Smith to slow the *Titanic* after receiving ice warnings [although to maintain speed was standard practice at the time – see the British Inquiry conclusion below]. However, perhaps the strongest criticism was levied at Captain Lord and the *Californian*. The committee found that the ship was, 'Nearer the *Titanic* than the 19 miles reported by her Captain, and that her officers and crew saw the distress signals of the *Titanic* and failed to respond to them in accordance with the dictates of humanity, international usage, and the requirements of law.'[15]

The British Inquiry concluded that:

> For … a quarter of a century or more, the practice of liners using this track when in the vicinity of ice at night had been, in clear weather, to keep the course, to maintain the speed and to trust to a sharp look-out to enable them to avoid the danger. This practice … had been justified by experience, no casualties having resulted from it … But the event has proved the practice to be bad. Its root is probably to be found in competition and in the desire of the public for quick passages rather than in the judgment of navigators …
>
> In these circumstances I am not able to blame Captain Smith. He … was doing only that which other skilled men would have done in the same position … The evidence shows that he was not trying to make any record passage or indeed any exceptionally quick passage … He made a mistake, a very grievous mistake, but one in which, in face of the practice and of past experience, negligence cannot be said to have had any part; and in the absence of negligence it is, in my opinion, impossible to fix Captain Smith with blame. It is, however, to be hoped that the last has been heard of the practice and that for the future it will be abandoned for what we now know to be more prudent and wiser measures. What was a mistake in

> the case of the *Titanic* would without doubt be negligence in any similar case in the future.[16]

One good thing did come out of the terrible *Titanic* tragedy. As a result of the Inquiries' recommendations, the first Convention on the Safety of Life at Sea (SOLAS) met in London on 12 November 1913. As Dave Gittins writes in *Report into the Loss of the SS Titanic* (from which the SOLAS articles and regulations reproduced here are taken), 'The ghost of the *Titanic* hovered near and the convention felt her influence.'[17]

Even before the SOLAS Convention, an International Radiotelegraphic Convention was held in London in 1912. Its proposals were complex but essentially:

> All ocean-going ships on international voyages with more than fifty people on board *must* [my italics] maintain a continuous wireless service [i.e., employ at least two trained Radio Operators].
>
> If a ship carried fewer than fifty people it could travel with only one Radio Operator but it must install an automatic signal-detecting alarm for use outside working hours to wake the sleeping Operator.

If the Radiotelegraph Convention's proposals had been in force when *Titanic* sailed, it's possible that many more would have survived because the *Californian*'s Marconi Operator, Cyril Evans, would have had a signal-detecting alarm that would have woken him, even though his Captain didn't.

The chief SOLAS articles were (I've paraphrased):

International support for the May 1912 Ice Patrol and definition of its duties. One duty was to report ice that was likely to endanger shipping. SOLAS Article 10: When ice is reported, the Captain must proceed at a moderate speed or alter course to clear the danger zone.

SOLAS Articles 29 & 30: Member nations must develop improved watertight designs.
SOLAS Article 40: A ship *may not travel* [my italics] with a total number of people greater than that for whom there are lifeboats and pontoon life rafts.
SOLAS Article 56: Crews must be informed of their emergency stations and duties before sailing.

The articles and regulations were signed on 20 January 1914 but they weren't ratified by governments of the participating nations until the 1920s, because the First World War intervened. Even so, by the 1920s formal training in lifeboat operation had begun and, 'boats or rafts for all' at last became the norm.

Two major changes came into force much more quickly, in 1912 and 1913:

> The Ice Patrol began work in May 1912.
> The International Radiotelegraph Convention was ratified by Britain in July 1913.[18]

So the *Titanic* disaster sowed the seeds for major changes to maritime safety regulations.[19] Although, inevitably, compliance with the changes sometimes *caused* disaster: when the SS *Eastland* fitted the newly required number of lifeboats to comply with the 1915 Seamen's Act, the extra weight added to her existing top-heaviness and caused her to sink after capsizing.[20] And it's a poignantly prescient fact that Emil Taussig – husband and father of two women who survived in Lifeboat Number 8 – wrote letters to the United States Steamship Inspection Service urging the enforcement of regulations to compel steamships to carry enough lifeboats for every passenger and crew member in case of accident, in 1908 and 1909,[21] three and four years before *Titanic* left Southampton. Taussig died when *Titanic* sank.

He wrote:

> It will certainly be calamitous if at the next disaster, which may occur, any of the passengers have lost their lives simply because there were not enough lifeboats for them to get into. That is a responsibility that nobody would be willing to shoulder. [But] ... Just as sure as you are living, and just as sure as there is a sun above us, this thing will come to pass sooner or later, unless the rules are amended compelling steamships to carry more boats.[22]

Captain Edward Smith and Thomas Andrews went down with the ship, so they could not speak for themselves, but *Titanic*'s owners, the White Star Line, used the law to allow them to avoid admitting any wrongdoing or negligence. The only person who successfully sued the White Star Line for the death of his son, Patrick, on board *Titanic* was Thomas Ryan, in 1913. Not only did Ryan achieve justice, but his case set a precedent in consumer contract law that protected rights for passengers.[23]

But that came later.

As if their suffering from the disaster hadn't done enough harm, *Titanic*'s survivors also suffered indignity, hurt and even more loss from the White Star Line's failure to meet their insurance claims with anything like adequate compensation. In May 1912, Lloyd's of London paid the White Star Line £1 million – the amount *Titanic* was insured for (approximately £133.5 million in 2025) – within thirty days of the sinking.[24] *Titanic* was under-insured (she cost £1.5 million to build – £200.3 million in 2025),[25] so the White Star Line didn't receive enough compensation to replace her.[26] Even so, the payment they received represented one-seventh of Lloyd's total underwriting for 1912.[27] But individual claims from *Titanic*'s survivors took years to settle and the amounts paid out were far less than claimed, with the exception of Thomas Ryan's case.

Noël Rothes and Gladys Cherry were lucky enough (or, in Noël's case, rich enough) to have paid for personal travel insurance with Thomas Cook, which paid out £100 each (£13,350 in 2025) and, as Noël's husband wrote to her parents from New York, 'T. Cook

… have written about Noël's insurance on jewels'. He didn't say whether or not T. Cook had or would pay for the loss of her jewellery but in *The Ship of Dreams*, Gareth Russell records a claim made by Noël against the Oceanic Steam Navigation Company (owned by the International Mercantile Marine Company, better known as the White Star Line) for the loss of her jewellery,[28] which is listed on the *Titanic Inquiry Project*'s Limitation of Liability Hearings pages.[29] Noël's claim was also for clothes and amounted to an eyewatering total of £2,485 (£331,800 in 2025). See the table below.[30]

Schedule 'A'.
Itemized List of Property Lost in Steamship '*Titanic*' on April 14th, 1912, By Countess of Rothes.

Jewelry Put in Charge of Purser: Market Value as of April 14th, 1912.	
1 Diamond Marquise Ring	£ 200
1 Large Diamond & Ruby Ring	£ 150
1 Small Diamond & Ruby Ring	£ 100
1 Diamond Ring	£ 60
1 Pearl Ring	£ 50
1 Emerald Ring	£ 130
1 Diamond Butterfly Brooch	£ 160
1 Diamond Spray Brooch	£ 150
1 Small Diamond & Pearl Brooch	£ 50
1 Emerald & Diamond Brooch	£ 70
3 prs. Ear-rings – 1 Diamond & Pearl & 2 Amethyst ditto	£ 130
1 Diamond Drop Necklace	£ 200
1 Diamond Buckle	£ 300
1 Paste Buckle	£ 15

In Dressing Bag:	
Silver Fittings with gold brooches - clock, etc.	£ 120
In 1 Big Trunk:	
Dresses from Loyse, 11, Princes Street, Hanover Sq., London; Underclothing – Woollands, Knightsbridge, London; Furs – Ermine and Seal and Black Fox – old lace inherited	£ 500
In 2 Small Cabin Trunks and 1 Hat Box:	
Hat box – hats £30 from Zyrots & Henry, London. Small cabin boxes boots and shoes – Hook & Knowles, Bond Street, London More underlinen and linen dresses and coats and skirts from Francis, 10 Grafton Street, London Feather boas, motor veils, gloves, etc. and fans – practically everything new	£ 100
TOTAL	£2,485

Noël Rothes' claim against the Oceanic Steam Navigation Company (owners of the White Star Line) for jewellery and clothes. (Courtesy of the *Titanic Inquiry Project*, Limitation of Liability Hearings page)

I don't know if Noël received any kind of compensation from the White Star Line, but I doubt it because she's not listed among the claimants on the American *Titanic* Inquiry's Limitation of Liability Hearings, Final Decree, 1916, where it states, above the long list of claimants:

> WHEREAS, on the return of the monition [cautionary advice] aforesaid, April 15, 1913, proclamation was duly made citing all persons claiming damages as aforesaid to appear and present their claims and to answer the petition herein, and *no person or persons other than those herein mentioned have presented claims, appeared or answered, or requested further time within which to file claims or to appear and answer the petition* [my italics].[31]

Only those with private insurance received anything like adequate compensation for damages, loss of property or loss of life claimed, through life insurance, by the families of the dead. The survivors who claimed against the Oceanic Steam Navigation Company for damages and loss of property received minimal amounts compared with their claims. They filed multiple lawsuits in the District Court for the Southern District of New York in 1913, asking for over $16 million ($375 million in 2025) in compensation for loss and injuries[32] as well as payments for negligence, but the American Supreme Court applied the Limited Liability Act and capped the damages.

The case settled in July 1916. The White Star Line paid out just $664,000 ($22.2 million in 2025). Claimants – including thirteen from Lifeboat Number 8 – never received any kind of admission of wrongdoing or acceptance of responsibility for the trauma they'd suffered *and* they had to agree that the company had no knowledge of any negligence on board before they were awarded their minimal damages.[33] (The only exception was the later Thomas Ryan case.) Claimants also had to agree to end their claims in America and in Britain. The list of claimants and/or family members claiming for their dead that appears in the *Titanic Inquiry Project*'s pages on the Limitation of Liability Hearings, Final Decree, includes this paragraph:

> It is ORDERED, ADJUDGED AND DECREED, that the collision of the steamship *Titanic* with an iceberg on April 14, 1912, and the subsequent sinking and loss of said steamship on April 15, 1912, and the losses, damages, injuries, destruction and fatalities resulting therefrom *were occasioned and incurred without the privity or knowledge of the petitioner [the White Star Line], and that the petitioner is not liable to any extent for any loss, damage, injury, destruction or fatality, or for any claim whatsoever in any way resulting or arising from or growing out of said collision and sinking and is free from all personal or corporate liability [until the Ryan case]*[34] [my italics] for any and all loss, damage, injury, destruction and fatality and claims resulting

> or arising from or growing out of said collision and sinking, as well as for any and all debts, claims and demands of whatsoever nature resulting or arising from or growing out of the voyage of the steamship *Titanic* which began at Southampton April 10, 1912.[35]

Noël boarded Lifeboat Number 8 wearing one piece of jewellery: a string of Scottish freshwater pearls. She wore them all the time because her husband gave them to her for their wedding. The rest of her jewellery (see pages 135–136) went down with the ship. When she met the purser, Hugh McElroy, on her way to the boat deck, he thanked her for not asking him to open the safe to give her the rest of her jewellery the way other people had.

British and American *Titanic* Relief Funds were set up immediately after the disaster (there were others, later on), which raised more than $2,250,000 and $161,000 respectively for the survivors and the families of the dead ($75.1 million and $5.4 million in 2025);[36] in Britain, George V gave 5,000 guineas (£701,100 in 2025) and parish councils and many other groups gave as much as they could afford.[37] Concerts were also put on in both countries to raise money, but these funds were the survivors' only immediate source of financial relief. Their claims against the White Star Line were capped by the Limited Liability Act and their right to appeal was non-existent.

In my opinion, it is unconscionable that *Titanic*'s owners were compensated by Lloyd's for two-thirds of the cost of their ship within a month of the sinking, but not a single passenger, let alone the families of those who died, were compensated properly (unless they could afford private insurance). I think it's equally unconscionable that *Titanic*'s wreck is a place trophy hunters visit to bring back memorabilia that fetches ludicrously large sums of money. The sinking caused the deaths of 1,496 people, so I feel strongly that the place where they died should remain a memorial sacred to them and *Titanic* artefacts should remain on the seabed with the wreck.

Titanic's position on the seabed, about 325 nautical miles (600km) south-south-east of the coast of Newfoundland, has been known since 1985 when a joint Franco-American expedition led by Dr Robert D. Ballard and Dr Jean-Louis Michel found her.[38] They were actually searching for two Cold War nuclear submarines, but when they found *Titanic* they saw that she'd broken apart as she sank: her bow and her stern lay on the seabed separated by some 2,000ft (600m).[39] The 2025 film *Titanic: A Digital Resurrection* states that her stern and bow are separated by 'a third of a mile'.[40]

Titanic came under UNESCO protection in 2012[41] and in January 2020 a British and American treaty was signed designating the site of the wreck a resting place for all who died, a place to be preserved and treated with sensitivity and respect. Any divers planning to explore the wreck must have a licence and both governments hold the power to grant or deny licences to remove artefacts.[42] Because *Titanic* lies in international waters, the wreck wasn't protected by law before 2012.

On the subject of laws, if those outlined on pages 132–133 had been in force when *Titanic* steamed away from Southampton on Wednesday, 10 April 1912, perhaps she wouldn't ever have been fatally wounded by the iceberg. Perhaps.

Sometime after the disaster, Bruce Ismay said:

> Everybody learns by experience. One thing that I learned when the *Titanic* went down is that the laws relating to the preservation of life are not adequate. They were based, no doubt, on the assumption that the great ocean liners, with their highly developed system of bulkheads, were unsinkable. But experience has taught us that at present there is no such thing as an unsinkable ship. I admit that I was among those who were deluded on this point.[43]

Ten

The Aftermath

They were brave men all that stood back so the women should have at least a chance to live[1]

The telegram on page 142 was sent by Alice Reeves to May Goodman (birth name Reeves) and her husband George. It arrived at Shearfold Farm in Sussex on 16 April 1912, so news of Noël's safety reached England very quickly, the day after *Titanic* sank (thirty-two and a half hours to be exact), even though she sent four Marconigrams from the *Carpathia* to her husband in New York, 'not one of which he received'.[2] It's likely that the Marconigram she sent her parents – that she talks about in her letter to them (see page 98) – didn't arrive either: I've seen a telegram from her father imploring the White Star Line for news.

May Goodman was Noël's first cousin and lifelong friend; she was six years older than Noël but they were both only children and they thought of each other as sisters. Alice Reeves was May's paternal aunt; Thomas Dyer-Edwardes (Noël's father) was May's maternal uncle. May and George Goodman would have wired Noël's parents – who were in France – to tell them their daughter was safe just as soon as they received the telegram.

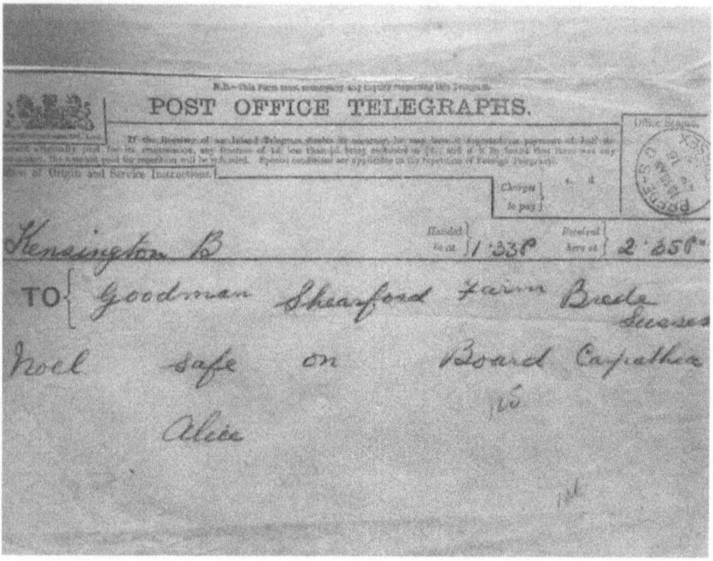

POST OFFICE TELEGRAPHS.

Kensington B

TO Goodman Shearford Farm Brede Sussex

Noel safe on Board Carpathia

Alice

Telegram confirming Noël's safety. It arrived in England very quickly (16 April at 10.50 a.m.). Some telegrams never arrived. This one was sent by Alice Reeves to May Goodman: Alice was May's paternal aunt, May was Noël's first cousin and lifelong friend. (Image courtesy of Joanna Hitchcock, May Goodman's granddaughter)

Gladys Cherry wrote her first letter to her mother on board *Carpathia* on 17 April 1912, two days after *Titanic* sank. She also hoped a telegram had arrived. An extract from her letter follows:

> I … hope you … got my Marconi, but the official messages had to be got off first, there were such dozens of these that they had to go in turn. We have been on here [*Carpathia*] since Monday at 8.30 [a.m.] when we were picked up and I have not been able to write a line before, it has all been too ghastly and I seem still dazed … its [sic] all too terrible … . It was beginning to get rough and very difficult to steer, I was numb from the waist downwards … we were pulled up in a hoist – like a swing. Nöel

> [sic] went up just before me, I could not walk when I got up as my legs had got numb, they took us all into the Saloon … . Then all the women came in some unconscious, some hysterical and all more of [sic] less collapsed, they had brandy for us, and hot coffee, and they were wonderful all they did for us; … – they have managed accommodation for us all here, with lots sleeping on the floor in the dining saloon; we have a cabin with four of us in, but we are thankful to be in anything.
>
> My nerves are all to pieces, and we are in a dense fog at present, we ought to get to New York tomorrow … its [sic] all been too ghastly, I can't blame anyone and they say the Captain shot himself [this is a rumour; it's thought one officer might have shot himself (and/or others) but the details remain unknown].[3] … Why did we go at that pace when they knew we were near ice bergs? … . The separating of husbands and wives was ghastly, Nöel [sic] and I are so thankful we had no man with us … our women … are wonderful – Mrs. Tyrrell Cavendish is here but the husband gone.[4]

On 23 April 1912, *The Morning Post* published a notice from Noël's parents. It was one of the many press cuttings found in her box of *Titanic* papers after she died. They'd clearly been overwhelmed with letters of sympathy for her safety:

> Mr. and Mrs. Dyer Edwardes find it impossible to reply personally to the many most kind and sympathetic letters and telegrams they have received concerning the merciful preservation of their only child, the Countess of Rothes, in the *Titanic* disaster.

On 26 April 1912, a week after arriving in New York, Noël wrote to May Goodman in England. She said that when *Carpathia* docked in New York her husband 'looked awful … poor darling'. She said, of the people waiting on the dock, 'You never saw anything so impressive as the huge silent crowds.'[5]

There were exaggerations and rumours printed in the press about the tragedy, which is why, I think, Noël and Jones reluctantly gave their interviews, to counteract them. In *The Loss of the Titanic*, Lawrence Beesley wrote about one of the worst. He didn't name the paper except to say that it was a New York paper, but the article also appeared in the *Valentine Democrat* in Valentine, Nebraska, ten days after the disaster.[6] It imagined *Titanic*'s passengers reacting hysterically to the collision with the iceberg:

> 'Stunned by the terrific impact, the dazed passengers rushed from their staterooms into the main saloon amid the crash of splintering steel, rending of plates and shattering of girders, while the boom of falling pinnacles of ice upon the broken deck of the great vessel added to the horror … In a wild ungovernable mob they poured out of the saloons to witness one of the most appalling scenes possible to conceive . . . . For a hundred feet the bow was a shapeless mass of bent, broken and splintered steel and iron.'
>
> And so on [wrote Lawrence Beesley], horror piled on horror, and not a word of it true, or remotely approaching the truth. This paper was selling in the streets of New York while the *Carpathia* was coming into dock, while relatives of those on board were at the docks to meet them and anxiously buying any paper that might contain news. No one on the *Carpathia* could have supplied such information; there was no one else in the world at that moment who knew any details of the *Titanic* disaster, and the only possible conclusion is that the whole thing was a deliberate fabrication to sell the paper.[7]

Those sorts of articles fuelled speculation and myth about what happened as *Titanic* sank. In *Shadow of the Titanic*, Andrew Wilson writes:

> The sinking of the *Titanic* was so shocking, so negative, so alien to the securities of Edwardian society, that almost as soon

> as the disaster was reported, myths began to spring up like fragments of driftwood from the sea.[8]

A first-class passenger, May Futrelle, whose husband Jacques Futrelle died in the disaster, noted that the veracity of many of the news clippings was often questionable.[9]

Noël Rothes' sworn statement, her letters and her press interviews and Thomas Jones' press interview, his letters and his evidence to the American Inquiry set the record straight. Here is the full text of Noël's sworn statement (I've quoted short extracts elsewhere in this book). It was witnessed by the British Vice-Consul in Los Angeles and made at Altadena, California, in May 1912, when Noël and her husband travelled to California as they'd originally planned. They stayed with friends in Altadena, but they never did buy the fruit farm Noël talked about so optimistically in the interview with *The New York Herald* on 11 April 1912, before she left Southampton (see page 16).

This sworn statement is typed and in my mother's third album. I haven't been able to find the original.

Copy of a sworn statement by Noël Rothes, in the matter of an inquiry into the loss of the S.S. 'TITANIC'

UNITED STATES OF AMERICA	)	In the matter of an inquiry
STATE OF CALIFORNIA	)	into the loss of the S.S.
COUNTY OF LOS ANGELES	)	'TITANIC'

Noël Rothes, wife of the Right Honourable Norman Evelyn Leslie, Earl of Rothes, in the Peerage of Scotland, of Leslie House, Fife, Scotland, at present temporarily residing at Altadena, in the County of Los Angeles, State of California, being duly sworn, doth depose and say:

I was a passenger on the Steamship 'TITANIC', which sailed from England for the Port of New York on the 10th day of April, 1912: and occupied Cabin No 77 on Deck 'C', with my cousin, Miss Cherry.

On the night of the disaster I had retired to my berth and was awakened by a slight shock, and noticing that the engines had stopped, I turned on the light and on looking at my watch, found that the time was 11:45pm.

On opening my cabin door, I saw the steward who attended my cabin, and upon asking him what had occurred, was informed that the ship had been in collision with ice.

As we wished to see an iceberg, we went on deck and walked to the forward part where we could see the portion of the boat occupied by steerage passengers. The deck below was covered with ice, but we did not see the iceberg.

There was no disturbance or confusion among the passengers.

We were returning to my cabin, as it was very cold and dark, when the Purser appeared and directed myself and others to go below and put on life belts and warm clothes and then return to Deck 'A'. We did so, and returned to Deck 'A' with my maid. We went on the Port side. There were a good many people already there, standing quietly talking, and women and children were being put into the boats.

We walked along the deck to where the Captain was superintending the loading of another boat, which I found was life boat No 8, into which we got, with about 30 others; all women except one sailor, a steward and a cook.

The Captain called our attention to the lights of a steamer and as the boat was being lowered, he called to the seaman to row to the said steamer, leave the passengers, and come back for another load.

We drifted about 20 yards from the ship, and observing that there were only three men in the boat, I asked the seaman if I could help him by taking the tiller, so that he might row, to which he assented. I took the tiller, and called to my cousin to help me, and the men and some women commenced rowing towards the lights of the steamer.

When we had gone a short distance T. Jones, a sailor who was in charge of the boat, said he wished to go back, as our boat could hold 10 or 12 more easily. Jones was very anxious to return, but the other people in the boat were very strongly against it, saying that the suction would take us down and we would be swamped.

The ship was brilliantly lighted and was going down fast. We could see the lights going out in the rows of portholes.

The firing of the rockets from the steamer and the blowing of her siren was continued almost to the last.

I spoke to one of the passengers and said that I thought that we ought to return. She, however, demurred on the ground that we might be swamped and asked me not to say anything more about it, as it might result in a panic in our boat if the others heard that I advocated returning.

Seaman Jones said: 'Now, Ladies, if we are saved and any questions are asked as to why we did not return, you will please remember that I wanted to go back and would rather be drowned with the others than not return'.

The majority said the Captain's orders were to row for the lights of the ship towards which we were heading, and on that ground we ought not to return.

I saw two lights on the steamer we were heading for and once for a short time I saw a red light on said steamer.

The only lights on our boat were a lantern, which went out and could not be re-lighted, and a small electric light in a walking-stick. We endeavoured to keep in touch with two of the other life boats whose lights we saw, by showing our lights and shouting.

After steering the boat for a short time, I changed places with a woman who was rowing and continued rowing for the rest of the night and Miss Cherry steered until we reached the *Carpathia.*

At dawn we lost sight of the vessel's lights. I did not see any panic or disorder on the ship before leaving her. I saw her sink and think it was about two o'clock. We were some way off. As far as I know there were no boat drills during the voyage. I saw one boat launched and was informed that several others had been launched before I went on board life boat No 8.

The sea was very calm until a slight breeze got up at sunrise. We were taken on the *Carpathia* about 6.30 or 7.00 in the morning.

I do not know of my own knowledge any circumstances attending the casualty, loss of the vessel, loss of life, the measures taken to save life and vessel, or equipment of the vessel, or the extent of the damage caused, save as aforesaid.

Subscribed and sworn at the
City of Los Angeles, in the
State of California, this [not noted]
day of May, 1912, before me,

British Vice-Consul at Los Angeles, California

In the Paris edition of *The New York Herald*, on 22 April 1912, at the end of her interview, Noël movingly and selflessly praised the men who died when she said:

> They were brave men all that stood back so that the women should have at least a chance to live. Their memories should be held sacred in the mind of the world forever.[10]

She meant every single man, crew and passenger, including the engineering crew who worked to maintain *Titanic*'s power so the lights stayed on so the passengers could see their way up to the boat deck to board the lifeboats. This courageous maintenance of power also meant that Jack Phillips could keep sending Marconi signals for as long as possible. A 2012 article in *The Scotsman* reported:

> *Titanic*'s engineers died out of sight, fighting to keep the ship's lights, pumps, and communications alive until the very end, enabling the crew to help more than 700 passengers into the boats … 'Being in the engine rooms, they were probably the farthest away from the means of escape', [said] Gordon Masterton [2005–06 President of the Institute of Civil Engineering]. 'When ships go down engineers always reflect on the likelihood, rather than possibility, of escape. A very high proportion of the engine room did lose their lives. It's a reflection of the hazardous nature of the engineers' work, the unsung heroes in the bowels of the ship when disaster strikes.'[11]

But the watertight compartments were collectively taking on water faster than the pumps could manage.[12]

Thomas Jones praised Noël's conduct in his interview with *The Daily Telegraph* for the way she helped him when she took the tiller, when she rowed and when she did her best to comfort the terrified women in Lifeboat Number 8. But I think he should be remembered for what he said when the majority in his lifeboat refused to let him turn his boat back to help people struggling in the freezing water behind them. His desire to turn back was so strong he was prepared to drown with them if he couldn't save them.

Noël described her thankfulness for their final arrival in New York on 18 April 1912 in her interview with the *Los Angeles Examiner* on 16 May 1912:

> In a moment after the ship had been tied to the dock, I was with my husband. [Their twelfth wedding anniversary was the next day, 19 April, but she didn't say so.] Oh, the thankfulness that was in me then. I had been saved. The words did not seem to tell anything, but the feeling in my heart spoke volumes. Yet, I will never forget that out in the broad Atlantic is the grave of more than fifteen hundred heroes who died that others might live.

Noël devoted much of her privileged life to the service of others (see her biography on pages 169–172).

In her third letter to her mother, written from New York on 19 April 1912, Gladys Cherry wrote:

> At last I am here safe and sound, now it is all over one feels very tired but full of gratitude and thankfulness for all the dangers we have been through .... It all seems like an ugly dream .... we got into the Dock last night at 9.30 [p.m.]. After having a dreadful time coming up the river, with all the newspaper tugs that wanted to put Pressmen on board but of course our Captain would allow no one to board us but the Pilot. All these people meeting the boat stood under their names, all the officials standing in lines to keep back the crowds, motors by the million were waiting. The reports about the condition of the passengers that had got about were terrible, it was quite upsetting.[13]

And, in a wire to her mother, dated Friday, 19 April 1912, 1.15 from New York:

> I am here with Charlie [her brother] and am all right – am resting I am so tired. Thank God I am here.[14]

Noël's husband took her to the Plaza Hotel in New York, where they stayed until 11 May before taking the train to California. Norman Evelyn Leslie, known as Evelyn and formally known as Rothes, wrote to his father-in-law, Thomas Dyer-Edwardes, on 7 May 1912 from the Plaza:

> My dear Mr Dyer-Edwardes –
> Thank you for your kind letter – no words can express my thankfulness nor how proud I am of Noël – her pluck and presence of mind has been simply marvellous – people who were with her in the boat have told me over and over again – she is much better & is eating & sleeping pretty well – but she doesn't take any interest at all in anything but this – the Doctor says is all [sic] to do with the terrible shock & that it will take a long time for her to get over it. (Naturally.) He thinks that the change to California will do her a lot of good & the journey will not harm her in any way – so we are leaving here on Saturday next May 11th & shall arrive Pasadena on Wednesday May 15th. & our address there will be: - Whitefriars, Altadena, Pasadena, California, U S A
>
> Telegrams: - Whitefriars, Pasadena, California
>
> We shall remain there 2 or 3 weeks and shall return through Canada & arrive in England about 7th or 8th July – Gladys has got something into one of her eyes which has poisoned it & has to remain in, else she is very fit – I am taking Noël to lunch today with Captain Charles on the '*Lusitania*' (the ship I came over in) as she is most awfully anxious to see over her & Charles is such a nice man comes [sic] from Gloucestershire – It is a beastly cold wet day – & the weather here is most changeable one day very hot & another wet and cold – Charlie Cherry is acting with Lewis Waller in 'The Explorers' here tonight – 1st night which is going on for 2 weeks & we have a small party & are going to it – Don't think I will let Noël do too much. I will take the very greatest care of her in every way – Please excuse pencil as she is occupying the only writing table –

T. Cook & Sons have paid Noël & Gladys their £100 each insurance & have written about Noël's insurance on jewels –

With our very best love to you both –

Yours affectionately

Rothes[15]

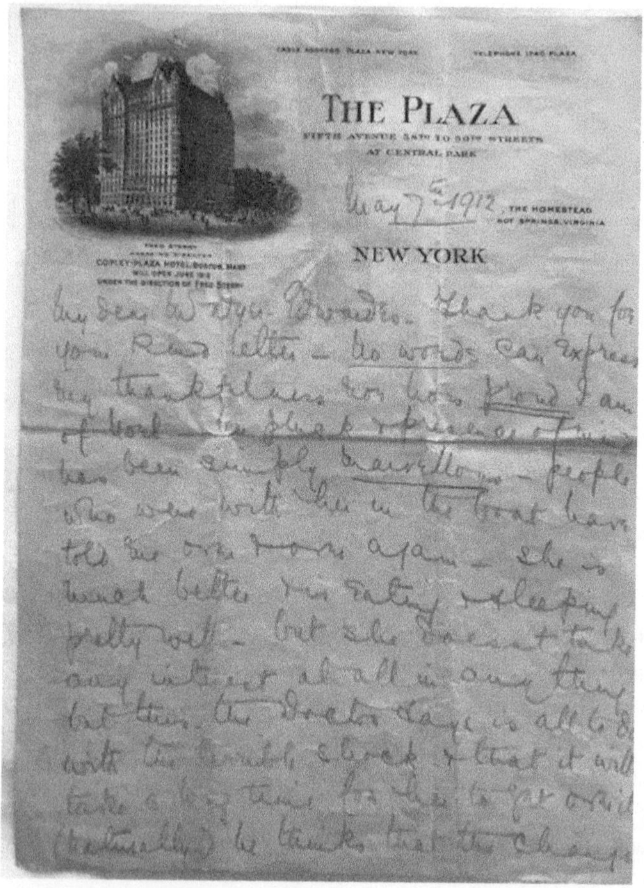
THE PLAZA

FIFTH AVENUE 58TH TO 59TH STREETS

AT CENTRAL PARK

May 7th 1912

NEW YORK

The first page of Evelyn Rothes' – Noël's husband's – 7 May 1912, letter to her father. He wrote the whole letter in pencil because Noël was occupying 'the only writing table' in their hotel room in New York. (Image courtesy of the Leslie family)

And here is the whole of Noël's letter to May Goodman, written from the Plaza Hotel in New York and dated 26 April 1912. The original is lost. Among other things, she wrote about how awful the press were:

> My dearest May,
> Thank you both for your wires; I send you just a few lines although I've been really pretty well until two days ago when I got a chill and have had to be in bed and am only just up again. The Doctor here is very fussy and won't let me do much as of course we are all feeling the strain a good bit now. If you ask Mother she will show you my first letter. I cannot write that awful description again and it would be difficult to explain to anyone how one still feels, all incapable of any emotion on the subject, one is so stunned with the horror of it all. I have the little Spanish widow [Maria-Josefa de Satode Peñasco y Castellana] here with me, she is wonderful, she knew no-one in America, but of course has friends now and clings very much to me: Her husband put her into my arms on the deck just before we got into the boats, and I promised to take care of her, I knew neither of them before. Its [sic] so cruel separating the men and women so much but one must obey orders or return to one's cabin, as Mr. and Mrs. Strauss [sic] did together [Isidor and Ida Straus]. Gladys [Cherry] was wonderful all the time and so was my maid [Roberta Maioni]. The Doctor won't let me travel yet as my heart is being tiresome, not serious, so write me a line here: Am getting some clothes slowly, of course we lost everything, except the few clothes and fur coats we had on. Luckily too for us lifebelts are warm things.
>
> The Press people here are really awful – one is never free and they are always printing imaginary interviews and photos of you which is maddening. I hope you are all flourishing? Am longing for more news of my boys – . How is your mother? [May Goodman's mother, Sophia Reeves, was the youngest of Noël's father's five sisters: Noël's paternal aunt.]

> Much love to you all, from Noël
> PS: R. [Rothes, Noël's husband] is very fit, he looked awful when we arrived, poor darling: You never saw anything so impressive as the huge silent crowds.[16]

In Noël's letter to Walter Lord for *A Night to Remember*, written forty-three years after the sinking in 1955, she is much kinder about the press than she is in her letter to May. But she wrote to May only eleven days after *Titanic* sank and the trauma she and all the survivors suffered would have been more than enough to cope with, without the added trauma of constant calls from the press to revisit the terrifying night in statements and interviews.

In a press cutting from *The Daily Telegraph* on 22 April 1912, found in Noël's box of *Titanic* papers, there's a report that Bruce Ismay wanted to leave America with all *Titanic*'s crew before the Inquiries began:

> Senator William Smith, of Michigan, a leading member of the Congressional Committee, was asked, before the first [Inquiry] session began, whether it was true, to his knowledge, that Mr Ismay sent three wireless messages ashore from the *Carpathia* directing the steamship *Cedric*, at New York, to be held, so that the surviving members of the *Titanic*'s crew could be sent back to England.
>
> Mr Smith replied: 'Why yes, of course. That is one reason why this hearing began so soon. A Government boat picked up messages stating that Mr. Ismay desired to sail on the *Cedric*, and they were forwarded to Washington. That made me take an early train to New York, and it was that which made me go to the pier on Thursday night [18 April 1912] when the *Carpathia* docked [at 9.30 p.m., according to Gladys Cherry]. Mr Ismay was anxious to go back, immediately. He wanted to go back on the *Lapland* on Saturday [20 April], and I had to tell him rather emphatically he couldn't go' … . The members of the Committee expressed their determination to call

> 'Every man, woman, or child' who can tell anything about the disaster.

Ismay was called to give evidence on the first day of the American Inquiry, Friday, 19 April 1912, as soon as possible after *Carpathia* docked. He expressed his 'sincere grief at this deplorable catastrophe', and said:

> We have nothing to conceal; nothing to hide. The ship was … the latest thing in the art of shipbuilding; absolutely no money was spared in her construction … . The ship never had been at full speed … . The *Titanic* being a new ship, we were gradually working her up. When you bring out a new ship you naturally do not start her running at full speed until you get everything working smoothly and satisfactorily down below … . She was going 75 revolutions … the day before the accident. That, of course, is nothing near her full speed.[17]

The SS *Lapland*, a Belgian Red Star Liner owned by the International Mercantile Marine Company, which owned the White Star Line, left New York bound for Plymouth on 20 April 1912, with many of *Titanic*'s crew on board.[18] But neither Bruce Ismay nor Thomas Jones were with them, even though Jones thought he would be when he wrote to his wife-to-be, Clara Moulton:

> Dear Clara,
> I am glad to inform you that I am alive after a great accident. There was a great loss of life. I was six hours in the water before we were picked up. I hope you never heard of it. I shall be glad to see you my dear again. I've lost everything but I still have my life. I will tell you about it when I return. I am coming home on the Red Star *Lapland*.[19]

I hope I would manage such graceful acceptance if I lost everything.

Jones stayed behind in New York because he'd been subpoenaed along with almost forty members of *Titanic*'s crew to give evidence to the American Inquiry. Of the subpoenaed deck crew, four were officers and nine were able seamen.[20] On the night *Carpathia* docked at New York, *Titanic*'s surviving crew were mustered on deck and ordered to the SS *Lapland* at New York's Pier 60, under an escort of officers. The next day, 19 April, the Women's Relief Committee brought clothing for the twenty stewardesses and $2,540 ($84,800 in 2025) to be divided among the men. More than 100 men and women took part in a poignant service to remember their fellow crew members; of the 891 who steamed out into the north Atlantic bound for New York, 679 were dead, including three women.

Titanic's seamen were designated Destitute British Seamen or those who 'cannot be deprived of their right to be taken home after shipwreck'. When the SS *Lapland* left New York, the remaining crewmen who were to appear at the Inquiry, including Thomas Jones, were housed at the Institute of the American Seamen's Friend Society, at 507 West Street near the Hudson River docks (where the service for their fellows had been held). They were given 'aid and comfort' by the staff, which included shelter, clothes and food.[21]

I thought Thomas Jones gave his evidence to the American Inquiry where it began, in New York, on 19 April, at the Waldorf-Astoria Hotel. But I've discovered that the hearing moved to Washington the following week[22] and Jones gave his evidence there, at the new Senate Office Building, on 25 April. He sent a postcard to Clara Moulton from Washington with a photograph of the National Hotel on the front. He wrote that that was where he was 'stopping'; he also bought a postcard of a photograph of the Senate Office Building. Both postcards were auctioned sometime towards the end of the 1990s: I've seen the auction record.

Jones returned to Southampton after giving evidence to the Inquiry and stayed for some months at the Sailors' Home there. His first letter to Noël is dated 28 June 1912 and his second, 29 September. Both letters are written on Sailors' Home letterhead but in August 1912 his name appears on the crew list for the *Oceanic*. So I think he must have stayed at the Sailors' Home after he returned from New York and then between voyages; he always worked the north Atlantic route that left from and returned to Southampton.

When Noël and her husband reached California she gave an interview to the *Los Angeles Examiner* on 16 May 1912, a month after *Titanic* sank. I've quoted from it elsewhere in the book. The full text follows.

Lady Rothes of Scotland, survivor of the *Titanic* disaster who, with the courage of a man, helped row a life boat during the night of the great tragedy, arrived in Pasadena yesterday afternoon.

Lady Rothes was accompanied by her husband, Lord Rothes. They will spend a month at 'White Friars' the beautiful home of C.M.M. Crichton in Altadena before returning to their home by way of Canada.

Lady Rothes gave to the 'Examiner' yesterday her story of the sinking of the *Titanic*. She told of the collision with the iceberg, the departure in the lifeboats, the bravery of men and women and, for the first time in Southern California, the story of how one life-boat pursued the lights of a departing ship in hope of succor.

She was a member of the crew of that boat which was sent out by Captain Smith to solicit the aid of a ship whose lights could be plainly seen. The story of the boat's dash into the dark waters after the will-o-the-wisp lights that faded gradually into the night, is probably the most impressive of the details on the part of the *Titanic*'s officers to secure help.

Lady Rothes Vividly Tells of *Titanic* Tragedy
Rows boat Through Dark Night Searching Aid

Lady Rothes, Heroine of *Titanic* Disaster, Who Arrived in Pasadena Yesterday. By Her Side is her Husband, Lord Rothes. These Titled Visitors Posed Expressly for the 'Examiner'.

Titled Scotch Woman, Survivor of Wreck, Arrives in Pasadena on Visit

Gayety Reigns Before Disaster

It was a faint hope that caused Captain Smith to send a boat load of thirty women with a crew of three men – a seaman, a cook and a steward, the latter two knowing nothing of handling a boat – in a mad chase after the distant light. During the hours that the small life craft pursued the larger vessel, Lady Rothes tugged at an oar.

Lady Rothes talked of the *Titanic* disaster in a way that showed that the hours following the wreck were forever graven upon her mind.

'The night of the collision was the most beautiful of the trip.'

Alone on Black Ocean

'There were no cries, no excitement, nothing save an occasional muffled sob from a woman who had left her husband on the *Titanic*'s deck. Some looked back to the great steamer which had been our ocean home; others peered ahead at the stern light of the steamer which knew or cared not of our peril.

'I can still see that stern light dimming, dimming, dimming until blackness came. Oh, that heartrending thought – we were alone on the ocean.

'Some of the survivors in our boat wanted to go back to the *Titanic*, but the majority feared the awful suction which would ensue should the steamer sink and doggedly we kept on our course, knowing not where we were rowing, but hoping that Providence would send us succor for the ones we left behind on the slanting decks of the sinking steamer.

'The end? Oh, I could not look. Some of those in our boat peered at the dying vessel, with half averted faces, for they knew what her going down meant. There were women with us who had husbands, sons, brothers and other male kin on that ship. They knew the exploding boilers sang a requiem.

'A shiver ran through us. Bitter cold smote us, but that did not cause the shiver. We knew death had crept upon hundreds of brave men and perhaps women had gone down, too.

'We were more than half a mile away when the *Titanic* went down, but we could not have saved anyone. All was darkness. We had no compass and to row for the spot where the ship went down would have been impossible. After the first great wail, all was tomb-like silence.

'In this terrible blackness we rowed all night. Bits of ice bumped the sides of our craft. It was cold. Our hearts seemed chilled, but we hoped against hope that some one would pick us up and arrive in time to save any who might be floating about the ocean. Terror did not come upon us at any time, we just hoped and were comforted in the hope that assistance would stem the march of death.

'When morning broke, we looked out on an ocean that had been the stage of a terrible tragedy. There was no ice about us. Nothing but water; no sign of the *Titanic* or any of the survivors greeted us. Alone. Alone.

'Up over the horizon came a black vapor. Eyes turned upon this beacon and hearts beat faster. It was smoke: it meant rescue. I cannot describe the feeling that came over me as I saw the masts, then the deck houses, and finally the hull of the *Carpathia* as she raced toward us.'

Saved by *Carpathia*

'Ours was the last boat to be picked up. As we boarded the *Carpathia* our little band of passengers first sought relatives or friends. Joy shone upon those who were successful in the quest and the woe of the disappointed ones was pitiable.

'How kind everyone was aboard that rescue ship. It seemed they could not do too much for our comfort. But there were some among us for whom they could do nothing: the kind hands of the *Carpathia* could not bring back lives.

'Again hope spread over the rescued. The word sped about that perhaps some other steamers had arrived in time to be of benefit. Up in the wireless room and among the ships officers the true story was known. Two words – too late.

'The survivors were dazed and shattered by the catastrophe. The journey to land seemed interminable. I sent four Marconigrams to Lord Rothes, not one of which he received.

'In the book of heroes the name of Captain Rostron of the *Carpathia* should be written. His steamer, the speed of which was not rated at more than 13 knots an hour, he drove through the night at 17 knots [now thought to be rated at 14 and travelling at 15 knots].[23] Captain Rostron handled the rescue work with the utmost skill.'

Awe Rules Great Throng

'We neared New York. Evening had fallen as we drew into the dock and peered over the ship's rail for our loved ones. That great throng had gathered, some seeking news of relatives aboard the *Titanic*, others to greet survivors, others were there merely out of curiosity. With bowed heads they stood, and from their throats came no cheers, no cries, no words. Awe ruled the throng.

'In a moment after the ship had been tied to the dock, I was with my husband. Oh, the thankfulness that was in me then. I had been saved. The words did not seem to tell anything, but the feeling in my heart spoke volumes. Yet, I will never forget that out in the broad Atlantic is the grave of more than fifteen hundred heroes who died that others might live.'

'What is your opinion of Mr Ismay?' was asked.

'He has been unjustly criticised,' she answered. 'As near as I can ascertain there were no women or children near when he went into the boat. He was not an officer or member of the crew of the ship and was treated with no more consideration than any other member of the passenger list.'

Lord and Lady Rothes are the parents of two fine boys, Malcolm, 10 years of age and John, two years old. Lord Rothes is the nineteenth Earl of Rothes, head of the Leslie clan and controls an estate of 10,000 acres in Scotland. Mr Crichton at whose home in Altadena they will reside during their stay in Southern California owns the estate adjoining the Rothes estate in Scotland. The Earl spent some time at the Crichton home in February, but this is the first visit of Lady Rothes to Southern California. She is a remarkably pretty English woman and is entranced with California even on so short an acquaintance.[24]

Titanic's sinking haunted both Thomas Jones and Noël Rothes. In an article published when Jones died in 1967, a friend remembered him saying that at *Titanic*'s end, 'We watched with tears streaming down our faces. Some of us prayed.'[25] In her letter to Walter Lord, parts of which appear among the sixty-three survivor stories documented in his book *A Night to Remember*, Noël wrote that, in 1913, she'd been dining out with friends and not thinking or talking about *Titanic* when:

> I suddenly felt the awful feeling of intense cold & horror that I associated with it all & I then realised the orchestra was playing *The Tales of Hoffman* [probably the 'Barcarolle'] which was the last music I heard played after dinner on the *Titanic*, tho' until that moment I had quite forgotten this.[26]

The original of Noël's letter to Walter Lord, dated 7 August 1955, is in the Caird Library archive at the National Maritime Museum in Greenwich. All the survivor letters written to Lord for *A Night to Remember* are lodged in that archive; they were donated to the museum when Lord died in 2002.[27]

Noël's letter is written in a rounded scrawl on small double-sided letterheaded pages just thirteen months before she died, forty-three years after *Titanic* sank, so some of what she wrote to her parents isn't mentioned there, and she added other things; for instance, begging Mrs Straus to get into Lifeboat Number 8 and the work she and Gladys did to help survivors on board *Carpathia*.

Only three survivors from Lifeboat Number 8 gave evidence to the Inquiries and all three are quoted in this book: Alfred Crawford, the first-class bedroom steward, gave evidence to both Inquiries,[28] while Thomas Jones[29] and Mrs J. Stuart White both gave evidence to the American Inquiry.[30]

When Noël asked Jones if there was anything she could do for him afterwards, he said the chapel he went to when he was a boy needed new paraffin lamps. Noël arranged for the lamps to be fitted at the Bethania Chapel in Tregele, north Anglesey. And now generations to come will remember Jones because, thanks to Eric Torr, the late Frank Egan, Linda Egan and Elizabeth Robinson of the Cemaes Bay History Group and Elfed Jones of Oriel Cemaes, a picture framer and gallery, there's a plaque to Twm (Tom) Titanic on the house where he was born in Cemaes Bay, overlooking the harbour. It was unveiled in 2023.

There's also a memorial to both Noël and Jones below Jones' house, on the edge of the bay (see page 163); fittingly, it's in the shape of the prow of a small boat and faces out to sea. There are engravings of Noël's and Jones' faces either side of an image of *Titanic*; the word *Titanic* graces its prow and there's an epitaph in both Welsh and English. The memorial was made, for his love of Cemaes Bay and its people, by Steve Blackwell of Blackwell's Stonecraft in Chester (he has a holiday home in Cemaes Bay). The memorial was unveiled in 2022.

The sinking of the *Titanic* changed lives irrevocably but, unlike the two heroes of this book, far too many didn't survive. Every 15 April the International Ice Patrol lays a wreath over the site where *Titanic* sank, in memory of all those who died.[31] The only good things to come out of the tragedy were the amendments to the regulations that governed Marconi wireless services on board

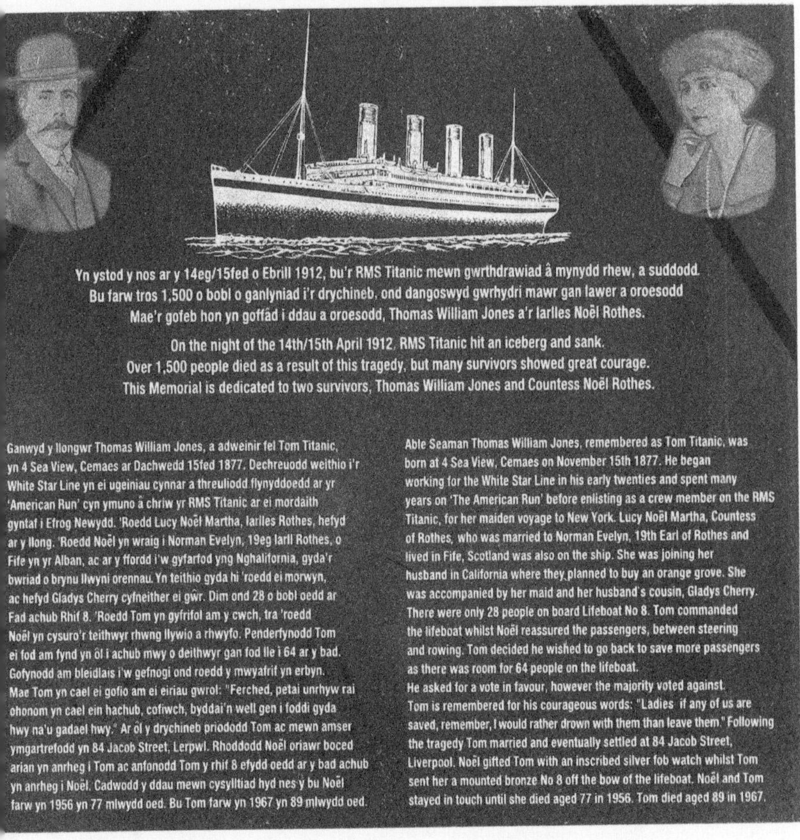

Memorial to Noël Rothes and Thomas Jones in Cemaes Bay, north Anglesey (Jones' birthplace). The epitaph is in Welsh and English. Made by Steve Blackwell of Blackwell's Stonecraft, Chester, and unveiled in 2022. (Image © Gareth Jones – no relation. Reproduced with his permission)

ship and the amendments to Maritime Law, which made life at sea safer.

I hope the way the aristocrat and the able seaman worked selflessly together on the night *Titanic* sank has inspired you as it continues to inspire me. I hope their stories and the way they highlight what went wrong, what shouldn't have gone wrong and what changed afterwards have enlightened you as they've enlightened me.

Theirs is a story of courage in the face of unthinkable tragedy: a story of two very different people who would never have met but for the disaster; two people who could never have imagined working side by side in a small lifeboat, at night, among towering icebergs for seven hours; but two people who worked harmoniously and steadfastly together; two people who did everything they could for the sake of twenty-five fellow survivors as they shepherded them to safety in Lifeboat Number 8.

Noël and Jones kept in touch until 1956 when Noël died but now, I hope, they'll be remembered by generations to come for their courage, kindness, resourcefulness, thoughtfulness, steadfastness and seafaring knowledge under, as he wrote to her, 'so terrifying' and 'so heartrending' circumstances.

Postscript

The *Lady Rothes*

A Thankoffering for Preserving the Life of my Only Child[1]

In 1915, in profound gratitude that the life of his only child, Noël Rothes, had been saved when *Titanic* sank, Thomas Dyer-Edwardes paid for a new motor lifeboat for the Royal National Lifeboat Institution (RNLI) at Fraserburgh in Aberdeenshire, Scotland. At its launch, on 4 August 1915, at the beginning of the second year of the First World War, he said:

> It is singularly appropriate that on this fateful day when the whole nation is pleading the sacred cause for which we are battling to Almighty God for aid and enlightenment, that we here at Fraserburgh should be engaged in launching this beautiful craft on its merciful errand. You doubtless all know why I am presenting this motor lifeboat to a port of Scotland, and why it should be called the '*Lady Rothes*'. It is a thankoffering to Almighty God for preserving the life of my only child from a great peril, in the foundering of the White Star Liner S.S. *Titanic*, a naval disaster only equalled by the dastardly sinking of the *Lusitania* by a German submarine … .

> I am not going to touch on the brave part Lady Rothes took during that awful experience, she has expressly forbidden me to do so. [But] It is not likely to be forgotten in Scotland where she bears an honoured and ancient name intimately connected with its history. But you may ask why was Fraserburgh selected .... I was informed that most, if not all the East Coast stations of Scotland were already supplied with lifeboats, Fraserburgh excepted. Leslie, the home of the Rothes is on [close to] the East Coast, so to Fraserburgh we came. Your storm-racked shore calls for such aid, and at a time like this, when our thoughts are turned daily to the awful destruction of life, and the devilish means ingeniously devised for its destruction it is a consolation to think that to-day we are engaged in launching a noble boat as a means of saving life from the perils of the sea.
>
> May the '*Lady Rothes*' through many a stormy winter to come prove herself capable of rescuing precious lives from an untimely death.

That report, from the 10 August 1915 edition of the *Fraserburgh Herald and Northern Counties Advertiser*, was found with Noël's press cuttings and is now in my mother's second album. It also said:

> The naming ceremony was performed by Lady Rothes who was accompanied by Lord Rothes, Colonel of the Highland Cyclists Battalion attached to the Black Watch, and by her father, the generous donor of the lifeboat.

The *Lady Rothes* cost Thomas Dyer-Edwardes £3,714 10*s* 5*d* (£401,500 in 2025). She was a 42ft self-righting Thames motor lifeboat. Her self-righting capability meant that, if she turned over in heavy seas, she would right herself in thirty seconds. A fitting 'thankoffering' from a father whose daughter's life had been saved in a lifeboat.

Ian Rothes, Noël's grandson, told Randy Bryan Bigham, a freelance writer, for his *Encyclopedia Titanica* article, 'A Matter of

The *Lady Rothes* lifeboat launched in Fraserburgh, Aberdeenshire, on 3 August 1915. Given to the RNLI by Thomas Dyer-Edwardes, Noël Rothes' father, in heartfelt thanks for her survival. (Image courtesy of Billy Watson, Fraserburgh RNLI. Originally published in the *Fraserburgh Herald and Northern Counties Advertiser*, 4 August 1915)

Course', that he thought the Fraserburgh lifeboat was her father's way of trying to soothe his daughter's 'Heartsickness at being unable to save anyone [any more] from the *Titanic*. That haunted her, I think, and must have been the great sadness of her life.'[2]

The *Lady Rothes* served the Fraserburgh community for twenty-two years between June 1915 and January 1937 and saved sixty-five lives:[3] the number that *could* have been saved in Lifeboat Number 8. Later, sadly, the *Lady Rothes* was discovered in a derelict condition on the island of Kerrera near Oban, but in the 27 March 1998 edition of the *Fraserburgh Herald* this headline appeared: 'The *Lady Rothes* is Coming Home today'.

Billy Watson, the Lifeboat Press Officer for the Fraserburgh RNLI, told me that 'Unfortunately, and frustratingly our lifeboat station kept no records from that period'. But he put me in touch with James Gray, joint Managing Director of Gray & Adams, manufacturers of temperature-controlled and bespoke vehicles, who told me that the *Fraserburgh Herald* and Kinnaird Radio enlisted his help to bring the *Lady Rothes* back to Fraserburgh in the late 1990s. He asked Fraserburgh Engineering to make a cradle – she was too fragile to transport otherwise – and J&G Forbes, boat builders, stored her at their boat yard in Sandhaven, 2 miles from Fraserburgh.

There were plans to set up a Lady Rothes Trust to fund the restoration. Ian Rothes, Noël's grandson, donated £1,000 and James Gray shared Rothes' opinion that the lifeboat should be restored as an onshore heritage monument and kept somewhere in Fraserburgh. But despite local excitement and planning, the restoration came to nothing and the *Lady Rothes* was sold. Sometime later she was discovered, burned. What was left of her was broken up and disposed of.

A sad end for a hard-working lifeboat.

But she did save sixty-five lives in her time.

Should this book make a profit, I plan to make a donation in memory of the *Lady Rothes* to the Fraserburgh RNLI.

Short Biographies of Noël Rothes and Thomas Jones

Lucy Noël Martha Leslie, Countess of Rothes, later Mrs Claud Macfie, 25 December 1878–12 September 1956

Lucy Noël Martha Dyer-Edwardes was the only child of Thomas and Clementina Dyer-Edwardes; her parents married in January 1878. They owned houses in London, Gloucestershire and northern France. Noël's father was a successful businessman, so her childhood was a privileged one. Ian Rothes, her grandson, recorded that they lived in Kensington, London, for the first ten years of Noël's life before moving to Prinknash Park (pronounced Prinnidge) in Gloucestershire. Her upbringing was conventionally Victorian, sheltered and strict, and always emphasised consideration for others. Noël was brought up to remember that many weren't as lucky as her and, in those days, privileged young girls were often taught by governesses, at home. I think it's fair to suppose Noël was educated that way.

Ian Rothes also recorded that, as an adult, Noël was small and slender, with beautiful blue eyes and brown hair. For much of her adult life Noël devoted herself to the service of others and in a vote of grateful thanks for her safe return from *Titanic*, the parishioners of Cranham and Prinknash Park wrote of their 'deep pride in her noble conduct, heroism, and absolute devotion to others'.

Occasionally her name was spelled Noëlle, but she always signed herself Noël and her name is spelled Noël on her birth, marriage and death certificates. She married Norman Evelyn Leslie, the 19th Earl of Rothes (pronounced *Roth*-iz: roth rhymes with moth) on 19 April 1900. They had two sons, Malcolm in 1902 and John (Jock) in 1909. In the early years of their marriage they lived in Devon before moving to Leslie House in Fife in 1904, when her husband inherited the Rothes property. But they were also often in London: after *Titanic* sank Noël wrote at least one letter to Thomas Jones from a flat in Albert Mansions.

In 1908 Noël helped raise money to establish the Queen Victoria School in Dunblane to educate children of the British Armed Forces; she also helped raise awareness of and funds for many, many charities throughout her life. Ian Rothes told Randy Bryan Bigham for his *Encyclopedia Titanica* article, 'A Matter of Course', about her 'charming way with guests, her laugh and her knack for getting money for her charities out of the hardest-heart[ed] cases'.[1]

In 1910 Noël helped establish a Voluntary Aid Detachment of Red Cross nurses at Leslie, called the Countess of Rothes VAD. In April 1911 a presentation of certificates for first aid and home nursing was made to its sixty members and, during the First World War, Noël turned the dining room at Leslie House, the family seat in Fife until 1919, into a VAD Auxiliary Hospital with ten beds, from August 1914.[2] Noël also served as a VAD Red Cross nurse at the Coulter Hospital for Officers in Grosvenor Square, London: there's a photograph of her in Red Cross uniform in the 24 July 1918 edition of *The Tatler*.[3] She also helped raise funds for the French Wounded Emergency Fund and, in the summer of 1918, she ran the Aunt Sally[4] stall at the Hurlingham Fête for Wounded Soldiers.

Noël's husband, Evelyn Rothes, served as Colonel of the Highland Cyclist Battalion at the beginning of the First World

Noël Rothes, centre, with her detachment of VAD Red Cross nurses outside Leslie House, Fife, Scotland, in August 1914. Noël turned the dining room at Leslie House into a ten-bed hospital. (Image © Robert Bogie Jarvis (d.1936); courtesy of Bill Fiet and the Leslie family)

War but that battalion was 'Raised to monitor our east coasts … they were never meant to be deployed overseas [and] by the end of 1915 … they were broken up'.[5] Evelyn's medal card shows that he embarked for France after January 1916, was wounded at the Battle of the Ancre on 3 October 1916 and subsequently entitled to a Special War Pension, which meant his wound was serious. He never fully recovered and died in March 1927.

In December 1927 Noël married Colonel Claud Macfie, her husband's greatest friend. They had a house at Kilmalieu, on Loch Linnhe on the Scottish west coast, and a flat in London, which was bombed in the Second World War. During that war Noël served with the St John Ambulance Brigade and, afterwards, she and Claud settled at Fayre Court in Fairford, Gloucestershire, where, in St Mary's Church, there's a memorial to them both. It uses the rare spelling 'Noëlle' and the dedication reads:

> Holiness is an infinite compassion for others. Greatness is to take the common things of life and walk truly among them. Happiness is a great love and much serving.[6]

Lucy Noël Martha Leslie, Countess of Rothes, later Mrs Claud Macfie, died of heart failure on 12 September 1956 at the age of 77.

Colonel and Mrs Claud Macfie in 1933. Noël stands beside her second husband, her first husband's greatest friend. They're clearly on a liner, but we don't know which one. She was 54. (Unknown photographer. Image courtesy of Joanna Hitchcock, granddaughter of May Goodman, Noël's first cousin)

Thomas William Jones
15 November 1877–16 June 1967

Thomas William Jones was the son of Griffith and Mary Jones (birth name Williams). An unsigned article claims that he had two brothers and a sister from his father's first marriage and an older sister and younger brother from his own parents' marriage.[7] Jones was born at 4 Sea View, Cemaes Bay (pronounced Kemus), north Anglesey, and his seafaring career began early: his first appearance on a crew list was in 1886, between January and June, on a ship called *Friends* registered at Beaumaris, 23 miles south-east of Cemaes Bay. He was listed as the ship's 'Boy': he was just 8 years old. The *Friends*' Master (Captain) was Griffith Jones, born in 1829: Thomas Jones' father.[8]

I think Jones joined the Royal Navy in 1891 at the age of 16 or 17. But I can't be sure because the records and crew lists don't show a naval rating called Thomas William Jones who was born on his certified birthday: 15 November 1877. There was a record for a Thomas Jones born on 12 September 1876 at Holyhead, Anglesey (by odd coincidence, 12 September was the day Noël died, in 1956, eighty years later), so Jones might have invented this birth date to make himself a year older in order for him to join the navy. If this record *is* his, he joined as a Boy Second Class, an entry-level rating, at 14. But to join at this level he should have been between 15 and 17 years old, hence the possibly invented birth date. And if this record is his, he served on the *Impregnable* and the *Lion*, and as Boy First Class (a promotion, but still a post for under-18s) on the *Boscawen*, *Vivid I*, the *Rupert* and the *RL Archer*, which foundered off Cape Flattery just north of Seattle in September 1894. The record states he was invalided out when he was 16.

By 1900 Jones was listed on the *Oceanic* as a fireman and in 1901 on the *Majestic* as a fireman (both were White Star Liners). I'm as sure as I can be it's him listed on these ships, but there were lots of Thomas Joneses listed who were born in Wales. By 1907 the crew lists show that he was definitely serving as an able seaman on board

Thomas Jones and the *Titanic* clock. Shelagh Oakes, Jones' granddaughter, sent this photograph. She doesn't know why her family called it the *Titanic* clock, but I wonder if Jones bought it with some of his *Titanic* service bonus? (See pages 28–29.) (Unknown photographer. Image courtesy of Shelagh Oakes)

the *Majestic*, and he said, in his evidence to the American Inquiry, that he'd served 'for six years without missing one trip across [the Atlantic] on her'.[9] Other crew lists show his service on *Majestic* in 1909, 1910 and 1911, with a promotion to quartermaster in August that year.[10] In early 1912 he was listed as a lookout, part of an able seaman's duties, on the *Oceanic*, and by 6 April 1912 he'd signed on to *Titanic* as an able seaman.

Shelagh Oakes, Jones' granddaughter, thought he never went back to sea after the *Titanic* disaster but I've discovered that he did. In August 1912, four months after *Titanic* sank, he was listed as quartermaster (promoted again from able seaman) on the *Oceanic*. He served on this ship in 1913 and 1914 and all his merchant navy service was on the 'American Run' or, more formally, the North Atlantic Mail Service, *Titanic*'s intended route. Jones served on the *Oceanic* until she was chartered by the Admiralty, on 8 August 1914, and converted into an armed merchant cruiser for war service. Her engineering and victualling crew transferred when the Admiralty chartered her, but it seems the deck crew didn't. Luckily for them, and Jones, because the *Oceanic* foundered off the Island of Foula, near the Shetland Islands, on 8 September 1914.[11]

After his last service on *Oceanic*, I think Jones stopped serving at sea because, by 1917, when his first child, Mary Ada, Shelagh's mother, was born he was described, on her birth certificate, as a landing-stage seaman. Shelagh thought Noël's husband, Evelyn Rothes, secured work for Jones on the Mersey Lightship, the BAR,[12] and certainly by the time his youngest daughter Ellen (Nell) was born in 1920, her birth certificate described him as a lightship seaman. A lightship acts as a lighthouse in dangerous waters and Jones' work was to make sure the light was always visible, to keep records of passing ships and to respond to emergencies. On his death certificate he was described as a dock gateman, retired, so his whole working life was dedicated to ships and the safety of their passengers and crew, whether at sea or from a lightship or from land.

Jones married Clara Moulton in 1916. Apart from their two daughters, they had a son, William Frank (Billy), in 1919. He was tragically killed in 1940 when his ship, the SS *Samala*, was torpedoed.[13]

Jones, Shelagh told me, was only 5ft 1in, but he was strong and he was, she said, 'Such a lovely man. A delightful man,' who never lost his Welsh accent despite living in Liverpool for most of his life. In 2021 a plaque was unveiled on the house at 84 Jacob Street, Liverpool 8, in Jones' memory. The family lived there for most of Jones' adult life, and he died there. Eric Torr, Chairman of the Cemaes Bay History Group, was instrumental in persuading Liverpool City Council to approve the plaque and at the unveiling ceremony one of Liverpool's City councillors said, 'Thomas Jones was an ordinary man who carried out extraordinary and unselfish acts.'[14]

Thomas William Jones died on 16 June 1967, also of heart failure, five months short of his ninetieth birthday.

Thomas Jones and his wife Clara at their eldest daughter, Mary Ada's wedding, 1941. Jones was 63. It was a bittersweet time: their eldest daughter was getting married but their only son had died in 1940 when his ship was torpedoed. (Unknown photographer. Image courtesy of Shelagh Oakes)

Acknowledgements

First of all, I'd like to thank Noël Rothes and Thomas Jones for their courage on the night *Titanic* sank. Without their quiet heroism this book wouldn't exist.

Second, I'd like to thank you, the readers of this book. A book can exist without readers, but it can't live without readers; it can't find its way out into the world of conversation and discussion and even, with any luck, recommendation, without readers. So, thank you.

Third, I'd like to thank The History Press for taking this book on without knowing anything about me as a writer (although they know much about *Titanic* from their numerous books on the subject). Thank you, The History Press, and especially Amy Rigg, Commissioning Editor, for publishing this *Titanic* story and for so patiently calming my anxieties and answering all my questions.

Many people helped and encouraged me. They corrected my mistakes (any that remain are mine and mine alone); they generously provided images and gave me permission to quote from their research; they tirelessly answered my questions and gave me new leads and connections. There are several families.

The archive and museum family: Anglesey Archives, the Antique Wireless Association, Linda Ballingall, the British Library, especially Lisa Kenny, David Brown, the California Historical Radio Society, the California State Library, Liverpool Archives, The National Archives at Kew, the National Library of Wales, the National Maritime Museum, the National Portrait Gallery, Southampton

Archives, especially Richard Arthur and the (amazing) *Titanic Inquiry Project*.

The Cemaes Bay family: Steve Blackwell, Carys Davies, Elfed Jones, Gareth Jones (neither are related to Thomas Jones), Eric Torr, J. Richard Williams.

The Goodman, Jones and Leslie families: Tessa Hardingham, Joanna Hitchcock (birth name Goodman), Alex and Miranda Leslie (birth name Grant), Fiona Mariota Leslie, the late Ian Leslie, 21st Earl of Rothes, Marigold Leslie, Countess of Rothes, the late Jean Mackenzie (birth name, Leslie), the late Eve Mackworth-Young (birth name Leslie), Shelagh Oakes, Hugo Sells, Lucinda Sells (birth name Mackworth-Young), Sue Tribolini.

The Titanic *research family*: Nick Barratt, George Behe, Randy Bryan Bigham, Mark Chirnside, Samuel Halpern, Philip Hind, Jon Kay, Daniel Klistorner, Tim Maltin, Lester J. Mitcham, Eugene Nesmeyanov, Rudi Newman, Robert Ottmers, Michael Pocock, Mike Poirier, Gareth Russell, Nicholas Wade, Christopher Ward, Claes-Göran Wetterholm, Andrew Wilson, Bill Wormstedt.

*The non-*Titanic *research family*: Belinda Braithwaite, Ken Carroll, Linda and Alistair Defriez, Bill Fiet, James Gray, Rachel Lee, James Leslie (no relation), Graeme McDonald, John MacKinnon, Billy Watson.

My writing family: the Barnes Bookshop, Kate Constable, Jody Cooksley, Sarah Jeans, Chris Lofts, Fatima Martin, Sola Odemuyiwa, the Society of Authors, Peter Wise.

And last but not least, Heather Holden-Brown for suggesting the idea for this book many moons ago (when I didn't write it); and Peter Wise for suffering my absence without complaint while I stowed away in my writing room at all hours of the day and night until this book was written.

Angela Young
August 2025

Notes

Introduction

1 American Inquiry conclusion: 1,517 died: www.titanicinquiry.org/USInq/USReport/AmInqRep03.php#a3
British Inquiry conclusion, 1,490 died: www.titanicinquiry.org/BOTInq/BOTReport/botRepSaved.php
The American and British Inquiries into the disaster, *Titanic Inquiry Project*,
BUT: 'The correct number of victims is 1,496 (and the correct number of survivors is 712). This figure was arrived at by four prominent researchers who independently went through the original passenger and crew rosters and counted each person, name by name. (All other numbers quoted in various *Titanic* writings are based on outdated information.) Modern research by the world's foremost *Titanic* passenger and crew experts confirm these figures.' George Behe, *Titanic* Historian and past Vice President of the Titanic Historical Society, April 2025, and Dr Rudi Newman PhD, Transport Historian and Author

2 Walter Lord & Nathaniel Philbrick, Introduction, *A Night to Remember*, Henry Holt & Company, 1955 and Griffin, 2005 (50th anniversary edition), cited here: https://en.wikipedia.org/wiki/A_Night_to_Remember; and John Welshman, *Titanic: The Last Night of a Small Town*, Oxford University Press, 2012, p.282

3 Mary-Clare Horn, remembering what her mother's cousin, Noël Rothes, said from time to time

4 Dr Rudi Newman, *Travelling to Tragedy*, PiXZ Books, 2017, p.41

5 Andrew Wilson, *Shadow of the Titanic*, Simon & Schuster, 2012, p.5

6 Thomas William Jones biography, *Encyclopedia Titanica*, www.encyclopedia-titanica.org/titanic-survivor/thomas-william-jones.html

7 BBC interview with Nell Jones and Angela Young, www.bbc.co.uk/news/uk-england-17583924

8 Transcripts of the American and the British Inquiries into the *Titanic* disaster, *Titanic Inquiry Project*, www.titanicinquiry.org/about.php

9 Arthur Rostron, Captain of the *Carpathia*, to the American Inquiry, *Titanic Inquiry Project*, www.titanicinquiry.org/USInq/AmInq01Rostron03.php

One: In the Beginning

1 Noël Rothes, interview, *New York Herald*, Paris edition, 11 April 1912, https://gallica.bnf.fr/ark:/12148/bpt6k4131416d/f1.image. With thanks to Philip Hind, Founder & Editor, *Encyclopedia Titanica*, for this link
2 The official inquiries into the disaster disagreed: the American Inquiry listed 2,223 people on board: 706 saved and 1,517 dead. The British Inquiry listed 2,201 people on board: 711 saved and 1,490 dead
3 George Behe, Samuel Halpern et al., *Report into the Loss of the SS Titanic*, The History Press, 2016, pp.67–70
4 *The Carolinian Newspaper*, 26 August 2024, https://caro.news/laroche-the-only-black-man-on-the-titanic
5 Leila Salloum Elias, 'Alien Passengers: Syrians Aboard the *Titanic*', www.palestine-studies.org/sites/default/files/jq-articles/JQ-52-Salloum-Alien_Passengers_2_0.pdf
6 Samantha Pak, 'The Six Chinese Men who Survived *Titanic*', https://joysauce.com/442-the-six-chinese-men-who-survived-the-titanic
7 Lester J. Mitcham, 1999–2001, www.encyclopedia-titanica.org/titanic-statistics.html
8 Noël Rothes, interview, *New York Herald*, Paris Edition, 11 April 1912, https://gallica.bnf.fr/ark:/12148/bpt6k4131416d/f1.image, with thanks to Philip Hind for this link
9 Arthur Rostron, Captain of the *Carpathia*, to the American Inquiry, *Titanic Inquiry Project*, www.titanicinquiry.org/USInq/AmInq01Rostron03.php
10 Dr Nick Barratt, Historian, *Lost Voices from the Titanic*, Preface Publishing, 2009, p.40, citing a Belfast observer in *Titanic: Death of a Dream*, Part One, https://archive.org/details/titanic-death-ofa-dream
11 Juliette Laroche, letter to her father, Kellie Carter Jackson PhD, Knafel Assistant Professor of the Humanities in the Department of Africana Studies at Wellesley College, *Untold Stories of the Titanic: The Only Black Passenger*, Noble Maritime Collection, 2022, www.youtube.com/watch?v=dzf1SVLAE74
12 Chantelle Francis, *New York Post*, 18 May 2023, https://nypost.com/2023/05/18/insane-image-reveals-titanic-compared-to-modern-day-cruise-ship, quoting an edited image posted on X, https://x.com/HistoricHub/status/1658593314059309057
13 From Thomas Jones' evidence to the American Inquiry, 1912, *Titanic Inquiry Project*, www.titanicinquiry.org/USInq/AmInq07Jones01.php
14 *New York Herald*, Paris Edition, 11 April 1912, front page, https://gallica.bnf.fr/ark:/12148/bpt6k4131416d/f1.image, with thanks to Philip Hind for this link
15 Dr Rudi Newman, *Travelling to Tragedy*, PiXZ Books, 2017, p.25

Two: Inventions and Invincibility

1 From Thomas Jones' evidence to the American Inquiry, 1912, *Titanic Inquiry Project*, www.titanicinquiry.org/USInq/AmInq07Jones01.php
2 www.encyclopedia-titanica.org/the-laying-of-titanics-keel.html, with thanks to Dr Rudi Newman for this information
3 Titanic Historical Society, https://titanichistoricalsociety.org/titanic-myths
4 With thanks to George Behe; also see Mark Chirnside, Maritime Historian and Writer, 'FAQ: Which Was *Olympic*'s Fastest Crossing?', *Mark Chirnside's Reception Room*, https://markchirnside.co.uk/faq-what-was-olympics-fastest-crossing; additional

updated speed information, from Mark Chirnside, https://markchirnside.co.uk/wp-content/uploads/2022/12/Article-Layout-Olympic-FAQ.pdf

5 J. Bruce Ismay, Chairman of the White Star Line, to the American Inquiry, *Titanic Inquiry Project*, www.titanicinquiry.org/USInq/AmInq01Ismay01.php

6 With thanks to George Behe

7 Testimony of Frederick Barrett, Leading Fireman, to the American Inquiry, *Titanic Inquiry Project*, www.titanicinquiry.org/USInq/AmInq18Barrett01.php

8 Blue Hill Observatory & Science Center handbook, Milton, MA, www.bluehill.org/handbook/Tables/Knots_to_MPH_Conversion.pdf

9 American Final Inquiry Report, *Titanic Inquiry Project*, www.titanicinquiry.org/USInq/USReport/AmInqRepSmith01.php, www.titanicinquiry.org/USInq/USReport/AmInqRepSmith02.php

10 Captain Rostron of the *Carpathia*, to the British Inquiry, *Titanic Inquiry Project*, www.titanicinquiry.org/BOTInq/BOTInq28Rostron02.php

11 Captain Rostron to the American Inquiry, *Titanic Inquiry Project*, www.titanicinquiry.org/USInq/AmInq01Rostron02.php

12 George Behe, Samuel Halpern et al., *Report into the Loss of the SS Titanic*, The History Press, 2016, pp.80–2

13 Senator William Alden Smith's Report to the US Senate, 28 May 1912, *Titanic Inquiry Project*, www.titanicinquiry.org/USInq/USReport/AmInqRepSmith01.php

14 Gladys Cherry, first letter to her mother, Lady Emily Cherry, written aboard the *Carpathia*, 17 April 1912; Hester Julian, *Memorials of Henry Forbes Julian*, Griffin, 1914; *Atlantic Daily Bulletin*; and George Behe, *On Board RMS Titanic: Memories of the Maiden Voyage*, The History Press, 2017, p.97

15 Lawrence Beesley, *The Loss of the Titanic*, Houghton Mifflin, 1912, www.gutenberg.org/cache/epub/6675/pg6675-images.html

16 Bruce Ismay, to the British Inquiry, *Titanic Inquiry Project*, www.titanicinquiry.org/BOTInq/BOTInq16Ismay03.php

17 https://en.wikipedia.org/wiki/Blue_Riband citing Arnold Kludas, *Record Breakers of the North Atlantic: Blue Riband Liners 1838–1952*, Chatham, 2000

18 Captain Rostron to the American Inquiry, *Titanic Inquiry Project*, www.titanicinquiry.org/USInq/AmInq01Rostron03.php

19 Grant R. Bigg & David J. Wilton, 'Iceberg risk in the *Titanic* year of 1912: was it exceptional?', *Weather*, Vol. 69, Issue 4, April 2014, https://rmets.onlinelibrary.wiley.com/doi/10.1002/wea.2238

20 Bruce Ismay to the British Inquiry, *Titanic Inquiry Project*, www.titanicinquiry.org/BOTInq/BOTInq16Ismay04.php

21 Noël Rothes, *New York Herald*, Paris Edition, 22 April 1912, https://gallica.bnf.fr/ark:/12148/bpt6k41314276/f1.image, with thanks to Philip Hind for this link

22 Gareth Russell, *The Ship of Dreams*, William Collins, 2020, pp.55–6

23 With thanks to Daniel Klistorner for his detailed analyses of *Titanic*'s cabins, costs and tickets. Further information from: Lester J. Mitcham, *Encyclopedia Titanica*, www.encyclopedia-titanica.org/community/threads/first-class-cabin-on-all-decks.5159

24 Daniel Klistorner, Ibid.

25 Lester J. Mitcham, www.encyclopedia-titanica.org/community/threads/third-class-cabins-price.5158

26 Antoine Resche, 'European Migrants' Crossings to the United States (1880–1925)', *Encyclopédie d'histoire numérique de l'Europe* (online), 2 July 2024, https://ehne.fr/en/node/14184
27 Paul Louden-Brown, *Titanic Belfast*, www.titanicbelfast.com/history-of-titanic/titanic-stories/titanic-food-for-all-classes
28 Ryan v. The White Star Line, BBC News NI, 18 April 2012: bonuses discussed at the end of the article, www.bbc.co.uk/news/uk-northern-ireland-17612629
29 'Five Ways to Compute the Relative Value of a UK Pound Amount, 1270 to Present', *MeasuringWorth*, 2025, www.measuringworth.com/ukcompare, and with thanks to Hugo Sells for pointing out that purchasing power comparisons vary depending upon whether a commodity, a wage, wealth or a project is being compared across years
30 'Why Did People Believe *Titanic* Was Unsinkable?', *History on the Net*, www.historyonthenet.com/the-titanic-why-did-people-believe-titanic-was-unsinkable
31 Claes-Göran Wetterholm, *Titanic, Ship of Dreams*, 2025 podcast, Episode One, 'The Biggest Ship in the World', https://www.bbc.co.uk/sounds/play/p0l49w26
32 George Jotham Hagar and Charles Leonard-Stuart, *Everybody's Cyclopedia v.5*, Syndicate Publishing Company, 1912, p.361, https://babel.hathitrust.org/cgi/pt?id=hvd.hn1qi6&seq=361
33 Guglielmo Marconi to the American Inquiry, *Titanic Inquiry Project*, www.titanicinquiry.org/USInq/AmInq01Marconi01.php
34 White Star Line Olympic Class brochure, 1910: quoted in several newspapers, including *The Shipbuilder*, with thanks to Dr Rudi Newman
35 *The Shipbuilder*, Midsummer 1911, p.26
36 George Behe, 'How the *Titanic* Became "Unsinkable"', https://wormstedt.com/GeorgeBehe/page2.htm?fbclid=Iw
37 With thanks to Dr Rudi Newman
38 Gareth Russell, *The Ship of Dreams*, William Collins, 2020, p.173, and https://en.wikipedia.org/wiki/RMS_Republic_(1903)
39 Sewell Chan, *New York Times*, 6 November 2009, https://archive.nytimes.com/cityroom.blogs.nytimes.com/2009/11/06/remembering-jack-binns-heroic-radio-operator
40 At 39 minutes, Dr Rudi Newman, *Titanic: Building the World's Largest Ship*, Channel 4, August 2024, www.channel4.com/programmes/titanic-building-the-worlds-largest-ship/; also in Dr Rudi Newman, *Travelling To Tragedy*, Halsgrove, 2017, p.11 (Olympic Class brochure) and p.13 (*Hawke*)
41 Captain Edward Smith, quoted in George Behe, 'How the *Titanic* Became "Unsinkable"', https://wormstedt.com/GeorgeBehe/page2.htm?fbclid=Iw
42 Jim Thompson, Harland & Wolff caulker, 1976 interview with BBC Radio Ulster, Dr Nick Barratt, *Lost Voices from the Titanic*, Preface Publishing, 2009, p.46
43 American Inquiry Final Report, *Titanic Inquiry Project*, www.titanicinquiry.org/USInq/USReport/AmInqRep05.php#a5
44 Julian Fellowes biography, www.britannica.com/biography/Julian-Fellowes
45 Julian Fellowes, *Titanic, Ship of Dreams*, 2025 podcast, Episode Two, 'Bad Luck Comes in Threes', www.bbc.co.uk/sounds/play/p0l49xt2
46 Tim Maltin, Author, Historian and TV Presenter, Ibid.
47 Thomas Jones, *Liverpool Echo*, 15 March 1956, p.4
48 Philip A.S. Franklin, US Vice President of the International Mercantile Marine Company, owner of the White Star Line, to the American Inquiry, *Titanic Inquiry Project*, www.titanicinquiry.org/USInq/AmInq03Franklin02.php

49 A *Titanic* deck hand to Mrs Albert Caldwell, Walter Lord, *A Night to Remember*, Longmans Green & Co., 1956, p.73

50 From Thomas Jones' evidence to the American Inquiry, 1912, *Titanic Inquiry Project*, www.titanicinquiry.org/USInq/AmInq07Jones01.php

Three: Luxury or Lifeboats

1 Noël Rothes, letter to her parents, Thomas and Clementina Dyer-Edwardes, written on board *Carpathia*, 18 April 1912. (Original lost. This text taken from a typed copy of the original, made in 1980 by Eve Mackworth-Young.) Courtesy of the Leslie family

2 The 1911 White Star Line Brochure for *Olympic* and *Titanic*, www.ggarchives.com/OceanTravel/Titanic/25-ImageLibrary/WhiteStarLineBrochure-OlympicAndTitanic-1911.html and 'Auction of a 1911 White Star Line brochure', *Belfast Telegraph*, 5 August 2022, www.belfasttelegraph.co.uk/life/rare-century-old-brochure-which-hails-the-titanic-the-epitome-of-security-expected-to-fetch-6000-at-auction/41517693.html

3 With thanks to Mark Chirnside; this research was first published in the British Titanic Society's *Atlantic Daily Bulletin*, September 2018, pp.28–9, https://markchirnside.co.uk/wp-content/uploads/2022/11/Titanic_Lifeboat_Increase.pdf; also https://markchirnside.co.uk/wp-content/uploads/2024/01/BigShipsSmallBoats1912.pdf

4 Mark Chirnside's talk, given at the Public Record Office Northern Ireland (PRONI) in September 2021, in a joint lecture programme between PRONI and the Belfast Titanic Society, *Olympic and Titanic, 'A Very Remote Contingency'*, www.youtube.com/watch?v=_w9-OZuIYjk

5 Ibid.

6 Ibid.

7 Anton Gill, *Titanic: The Real Story of the Construction of the World's Most Famous Ship*, Channel 4 Books, 2012, p.222

8 British Inquiry Report, *Titanic Inquiry Project*, www.titanicinquiry.org/BOTInq/BOTReport/BOTRepBoats.php

9 American Inquiry Report, *Titanic Inquiry Project*, www.titanicinquiry.org/USInq/USReport/AmInqRep07.php#a2

10 George Behe, Samuel Halpern et al., *Report into the Loss of the SS Titanic*, The History Press, 2016, pp.67–70

11 Ibid., p.169

12 John E. Hart, Third-Class Steward, evidence to the British Inquiry, *Titanic Inquiry Project*, www.titanicinquiry.org/BOTInq/BOTInq09Hart02.php

13 Antoine Resche, 'European Migrants' Crossings to the United States (1880–1925)', *Encyclopédie d'histoire numérique de l'Europe* (online), 2 July 2024, https://ehne.fr/en/node/14184

14 George Behe, Samuel Halpern et al., *Report into the Loss of the SS Titanic*, The History Press, 2016, p.67

15 Ibid., p.168

16 John E. Hart, Third Class Steward, evidence to the British Inquiry, *Titanic Inquiry Project*, www.titanicinquiry.org/BOTInq/BOTInq09Hart02.php

17 Ibid., first page: www.titanicinquiry.org/BOTInq/BOTInq09Hart01.php

18 American Inquiry Final Report, *Titanic Inquiry Project*, www.titanicinquiry.org/USInq/USReport/AmInqRepSmith01.php

19 *The New York Times*, 20 April 1912, p.8, www.nytimes.com/1912/04/20/archives/titanics-seamen-at-prayer-service-all-deeply-moved-many-weeping.html

20 From Alfred Crawford's evidence to the American Inquiry, 1912, *Titanic Inquiry Project*, www.titanicinquiry.org/USInq/AmInq01Crawford02.php
21 Senator William Alden Smith to the American Inquiry, *Titanic Inquiry Project*, www.titanicinquiry.org/USInq/USReport/AmInqRepSmith01.php
22 Anton Gill, *Titanic: The Real Story of the Construction of the World's Most Famous Ship*, Channel 4 Books, 2012, p.161, and Mark Chirnside, *The Olympic-Class Ships*, Tempus, 2004, cited here: https://en.wikipedia.org/wiki/Lifeboats_of_the_Titanic
23 Arthur Rostron, Captain of the *Carpathia*, to the American Inquiry, *Titanic Inquiry Project*, www.titanicinquiry.org/USInq/AmInq01Rostron03.php
24 George Behe, Samuel Halpern et al., *Report into the Loss of the SS Titanic*, The History Press, 2016, p.165
25 Records of the Board of Trade, https://discovery.nationalarchives.gov.uk/details/r/C38
26 From Thomas Jones' evidence to the American Inquiry, 1912, *Titanic Inquiry Project*, www.titanicinquiry.org/USInq/AmInq07Jones01.php
27 Noël Rothes, *New York Herald*, Paris Edition, 22 April 1912, https://gallica.bnf.fr/ark:/12148/bpt6k41314276/f1.image, with thanks to Philip Hind for this link
28 https://en.wikipedia.org/wiki/RMS_Olympic citing Hugh Brewster & Laurie Coulter, *882½ Amazing Answers to Your Questions about the Titanic*, Madison Press, 1998, p.78
29 February 1913 Blueprint, courtesy of Mark Chirnside, '*Titanic*'s Lifeboats: Fact & Fiction', *Mark Chirnside's Reception Room*, p.3, https://markchirnside.co.uk/wp-content/uploads/2022/11/Titanic_Lifeboat_FalseClaims.pdf
30 Noël Rothes, letter to her parents, Thomas and Clementina Dyer-Edwardes, written on board *Carpathia*, 18 April 1912. (Original lost. This text taken from a typed copy of the original, made in 1980 by Eve Mackworth-Young.) Courtesy of the Leslie family
31 Bruce Ismay, testimony to the American Inquiry, *Titanic Inquiry Project*, www.titanicinquiry.org/USInq/AmInq11Ismay04.php
32 Mark Chirnside, https://markchirnside.co.uk/about
33 American Inquiry, Final Report, *Titanic Inquiry Project*, www.titanicinquiry.org/USInq/USReport/AmInqRep05.php#a5
34 Bruce Ismay, American Inquiry, *Titanic Inquiry Project*, www.titanicinquiry.org/USInq/AmInq11Ismay03.php
35 Dr Rudi Newman, *Travelling to Tragedy*, PiXZ Books, 2017, p.21
36 Dr Rudi Newman, 'Another Rivetting Article ... – an Historical Rejoinder to Metallurgical Studies of the *Titanic* Disaster', *Atlantic Daily Bulletin*, September 2012, pp.18–30, www.academia.edu/2441774/Another_Rivetting_Article_an_Historical_Rejoinder_to_Metallurgical_Studies_of_the_Titanic_Disaster

Four: Leaving *Titanic*

1 From Thomas Jones' evidence to the American Inquiry, 1912, *Titanic Inquiry Project*, www.titanicinquiry.org/USInq/AmInq07Jones01.php
2 Lawrence Beesley, *The Loss of the Titanic*, Houghton Mifflin, 1912, www.gutenberg.org/cache/epub/6675/pg6675-images.html
3 Noël Rothes, *New York Herald*, Paris edition, 22 April 1912, https://gallica.bnf.fr/ark:/12148/bpt6k41314276/f1.image, with thanks to Philip Hind for this link
4 Marie Grice Young, 18 April 1912, George Behe, *On Board RMS Titanic: Memories of the Maiden Voyage*, The History Press, 2017, p.134

5 Dr Rudi Newman, *Travelling to Tragedy*, PiXZ Books, 2017, pp.21–2

6 George Behe, Samuel Halpern et al., *Report into the Loss of the SS Titanic*, The History Press, 2016, pp.132, 281, 282

7 Mrs J. Stuart White, evidence to the American Inquiry, *Titanic Inquiry Project*, www.titanicinquiry.org/USInq/AmInq12White01.php

8 Gladys Cherry, first letter to her mother, Lady Emily Cherry, written aboard the *Carpathia*, 17 April 1912; Hester Julian, *Memorials of Henry Forbes Julian* (Griffin, 1914); *Atlantic Daily Bulletin*; and George Behe, *On Board RMS Titanic: Memories of the Maiden Voyage*, The History Press, 2017, p.97

9 Senator Alden Smith's Report to the American Inquiry, *Titanic Inquiry Project*, www.titanicinquiry.org/USInq/USReport/AmInqRepSmith01.php

10 Lawrence Beesley, *The Loss of the Titanic*, Houghton Mifflin, 1912, www.gutenberg.org/cache/epub/6675/pg6675-images.html

11 Noël Rothes, 1980-typed copy of her sworn statement to the American Inquiry, made to the British Vice-Consul at Altadena, California, in May 1912

12 From Alfred Crawford's evidence to the American Inquiry, 1912, *Titanic Inquiry Project*, www.titanicinquiry.org/USInq/AmInq01Crawford01.php, and www.titanicinquiry.org/USInq/AmInq09Crawford02.php

13 Gladys Cherry, first letter to her mother, Lady Emily Cherry, written aboard the *Carpathia*, 17 April 1912; Hester Julian, *Memorials of Henry Forbes Julian* (Griffin, 1914); *Atlantic Daily Bulletin*; and George Behe, *On Board RMS Titanic: Memories of the Maiden Voyage*, The History Press, 2017, p.98

14 Noël Rothes, letter to her parents, Thomas and Clementina Dyer-Edwardes, written on board *Carpathia*, 18 April 1912. (Original lost. This text taken from a typed copy of the original, made in 1980 by Eve Mackworth-Young.) Courtesy of the Leslie family

15 Noël Rothes, letter to May Goodman, her cousin and lifelong friend, from the Plaza Hotel, New York, 26 April 1912. Courtesy of the Leslie family

16 George Behe

17 Dr Rudi Newman, '*Titanic*'s Boilers: A New Theory', *Atlantic Daily Bulletin* (September 2014), pp.13–15, www.academia.edu/25269010/Titanics_Boilers_A_New_Theory

18 From Alfred Crawford's evidence to the American Inquiry, 1912, *Titanic Inquiry Project*, www.titanicinquiry.org/USInq/AmInq01Crawford02.php

19 Victoria Brown, *The Death Ship: Recovering the Bodies of Titanic's Dead*, The History Press, 2025, pp.36–7

20 Fifth Officer Lowe's evidence to the American Inquiry, 1912, *Titanic Inquiry Project*, www.titanicinquiry.org/USInq/AmInq05Lowe07.php

21 George Behe

22 The British Wreck Commission (the British Inquiry), *Titanic Inquiry Project*, www.titanicinquiry.org/BOTInq/BOTReport/BOTRepBoats.php

23 Charles Bigham, Lord Mersey of Toxteth, British Wreck Commissioner, *Titanic Inquiry Project*, www.titanicinquiry.org/BOTInq/BOT01.php

24 Noël Rothes, letter to her parents, Thomas and Clementina Dyer-Edwardes, written on board *Carpathia*, 18 April 1912. (Original lost. This text taken from a typed copy of the original, made in 1980 by Eve Mackworth-Young.) Courtesy of the Leslie family

25 Caroline Bonnell, 18 April 1912, on board *Carpathia* and later, George Behe, *On Board RMS Titanic: Memories of the Maiden Voyage*, The History Press, 2017, p.163

26 Bill Wormstedt, Tad Fitch and George Behe, with contributions by Sam Halpern and J. Kent Layton, '[Lifeboat] Launch Times Re-Examined', https://wormstedt.com/Titanic/lifeboats/lifeboattable2.htm, with supporting information here: '*Titanic*:

The Lifeboat Launching Sequence Re-Examined', https://wormstedt.com/Titanic/lifeboats/lifeboats.htm

27 From Thomas Jones' evidence to the American Inquiry, 1912, *Titanic Inquiry Project*, www.titanicinquiry.org/USInq/AmInq07Jones01.php

28 From Alfred Crawford's evidence to the American Inquiry, 1912, *Titanic Inquiry Project*, www.titanicinquiry.org/USInq/AmInq01Crawford01.php

29 Ibid.

30 Caroline Bonnell, 18 April 1912, on board *Carpathia* and later George Behe, *On Board RMS Titanic: Memories of the Maiden Voyage*, The History Press, 2017, p.163

31 *Encyclopedia Titanica*, www.encyclopedia-titanica.org/titanic/lifeboats/lifeboat-8

32 British Wreck Commission, *Titanic Inquiry Project*, www.titanicinquiry.org/BOTInq/BOTReport/BOTRepBoats.php

33 Bill Wormstedt et al., '*Titanic*: Which People were in What Lifeboat, a New Study', 2025, https://wormstedt.com/Lifeboat_Project/Lifeboat_Project_Survivors.html

34 Second Officer Lightoller, BBC News, www.bbc.co.uk/news/uk-england-17614345

35 First Officer Murdoch, *Titanic's Officers*, www.titanicofficers.com/titanic_03_murdoch_09.html

36 Janet Dempsey, Maritime Records Specialist at The National Archives, *Women and Children First*, three minutes into her talk, https://media.nationalarchives.gov.uk/index.php/women-and-children-first, with thanks to Dr Rudi Newman for this reference, and https://en.wikipedia.org/wiki/Xhosa_Wars

37 From Thomas Jones' evidence to the American Inquiry, 1912, *Titanic Inquiry Project*, www.titanicinquiry.org/USInq/AmInq07Jones01.php

38 From Alfred Crawford's evidence to the American Inquiry, 1912, *Titanic Inquiry Project*, www.titanicinquiry.org/USInq/AmInq01Crawford01.php

39 From Alfred Crawford's evidence to the British Inquiry, 1912, *Titanic Inquiry Project*, www.titanicinquiry.org/BOTInq/BOTInq16Crawford01.php

40 George Behe, April 2025, citing: Samuel Halpern, *Strangers on the Horizon*, Independently Published, 2019

41 From Alfred Crawford's evidence to the American Inquiry, 1912, *Titanic Inquiry Project*, www.titanicinquiry.org/USInq/AmInq09Crawford01.php

42 Ibid.

43 From Alfred Crawford's evidence to the British Inquiry, 1912, *Titanic Inquiry Project*, www.titanicinquiry.org/BOTInq/BOTInq16Crawford02.php

44 Mrs J. Stuart White, evidence to the American Inquiry, *Titanic Inquiry Project*, www.titanicinquiry.org/USInq/AmInq12White01.php

45 Noël Rothes, interview, *Los Angeles Examiner*, 16 May 1912, https://libraryca.libanswers.com/loaderTicket?fid=4953037&type=0&key=0069c59eaf449530d9c46d6c39289348. With thanks to the California State Library for this link

46 *New York Herald*, Paris edition, https://gallica.bnf.fr/ark:/12148/bpt6k41314276/f1.image, and the longer version New York edition, www.encyclopedia-titanica.org/titanic-the-countess-of-rothes-and-the-phantom-light.html. The article was also syndicated – so, for instance, *The Monroe News-Star* published the longer version as well. With thanks to Philip Hind for these links

Five: A Fatal Mistake

1 Thomas Jones, interview with *The Daily Telegraph*, 22 April 1912
2 George Behe, Samuel Halpern et al., *Report into the Loss of the SS Titanic*, The History Press, 2016, p.199
3 James Gibson, Apprentice Officer on the *Californian* to the British Inquiry, *Titanic Inquiry Project*, www.titanicinquiry.org/BOTInq/BOTInq07Gibson01.php, cited by George Behe
4 *Titanic, Ship of Dreams*, 2025 podcast, Episode Six, 'Save Our Souls', www.bbc.co.uk/sounds/play/p0l9pp27
5 Tim Maltin, 'The hidden cause of the *Titanic* disaster', 5 January 2021, https://timmaltin.com/2021/01/05/thermal-inversion-titanic-disaster, also Tim Maltin, *Titanic: A Very Deceiving Night*, Malt House Publishing, 2012
6 Ibid.
7 Ibid.
8 Carl Kruse, 'Morse Code Revisited: Communing with *Titanic*'s Distress Signal, March 2020, www.carlkruse.com/morse-code-revisited-communing-with-titanics-distress-signal
9 Captain Stanley Lord's evidence to the American and the British Inquiries, 1912, www.titanicinquiry.org/USInq/AmInq08Lord01.php, and www.titanicinquiry.org/BOTInq/BOTInq07Lord01.php
10 Titanic Historical Society, Paul Louden-Brown, Edward Kamuda and Karen Kamuda, https://titanichistoricalsociety.org/titanic-myths
11 Cyril Evans, *Californian*'s Marconi Operator, evidence to the American Inquiry, 1912, *Titanic Inquiry Project*, www.titanicinquiry.org/USInq/AmInq08EvansCF02.php
12 Captain Stanley Lord, evidence to the American Inquiry, 1912, *Titanic Inquiry Project*, www.titanicinquiry.org/USInq/AmInq08Lord01.php
13 Cyril Evans, *Californian*'s Marconi Operator, evidence to the American Inquiry, 1912, *Titanic Inquiry Project*, www.titanicinquiry.org/USInq/AmInq08EvansCF01.php
14 Harold Bride, *Titanic*'s Assistant Marconi Officer, evidence to the American Inquiry, 1912, *Titanic Inquiry Project*, www.titanicinquiry.org/USInq/AmInq02Bride01.php
15 Captain Edward Smith to Quartermaster George Rowe, Walter Lord, *A Night to Remember*, Longmans Green & Co., 1956, p.98
16 Tim Maltin, 'The hidden cause of the *Titanic* disaster', 5 January 2021, https://timmaltin.com/2021/01/05/thermal-inversion-titanic-disaster, also Tim Maltin, *Titanic: A Very Deceiving Night*, Malt House Publishing, 2012
17 Harold Bride, *Titanic*'s Assistant Marconi Operator, evidence to the American Inquiry, 1912, *Titanic Inquiry Project*, www.titanicinquiry.org/USInq/AmInq02Bride02.php
18 Ibid.
19 Ibid.
20 George Behe
21 *Frankfurt* and *Titanic* communications (see also List of Ships' distances from *Titanic*; note 14 in Chapter Seven); https://en.wikipedia.org/wiki/SS_Frankfurt; additional information: Tim Maltin, https://timmaltin.com/2019/04/10/frankfurt-titanic
22 Harold Bride, evidence to the American Inquiry, 1912, *Titanic Inquiry Project*, www.titanicinquiry.org/USInq/AmInq02Bride03.php
23 Harold Cottam, *Carpathia*'s Wireless Operator, evidence to the American Inquiry, 1912, *Titanic Inquiry Project*, www.titanicinquiry.org/USInq/AmInq06Cottam03.php
24 Letter from Harold Bride, to W.R. Cross, Traffic Manager of the Marconi Company, 27 April 1912, LMQ/7/1/12, Caird Library, National Maritime Museum, Greenwich,

cited in: Dr Nick Barratt, *Lost Voices from the Titanic*, Preface Publishing, 2009, p.140, and here: *Titanic Inquiry Project*, www.titanicinquiry.org/USInq/AmInq14Bride01.php

25 Senator Smith on Captain Stanley Lord's culpability, to the American Inquiry, 1912, *Titanic Inquiry Project*, www.titanicinquiry.org/USInq/USReport/AmInqRepSmith02.php

26 Dr Rudi Newman and www.encyclopedia-titanica.org/californian-incident.html

27 George Behe, Samuel Halpern et al., *Report into the Loss of the SS Titanic*, The History Press, 2016, p.194

28 Captain Stanley Lord of the *Californian*, evidence to the American Inquiry, 1912, *Titanic Inquiry Project*, www.titanicinquiry.org/USInq/AmInq08Lord03.php

29 Lawrence Beesley, *The Loss of the Titanic*, Houghton Mifflin, 1912, www.gutenberg.org/cache/epub/6675/pg6675-images.html

30 From Alfred Crawford's evidence to the British Inquiry, 1912, *Titanic Inquiry Project*, www.titanicinquiry.org/botinq/botinq16crawford02.php

31 Noël Rothes' letter, 7 August 1955, to Walter Lord, for his book, *A Night to Remember*, LMQ/7/2/20, Caird Library, National Maritime Museum, Greenwich

32 Thomas Jones, interview with *The Daily Telegraph*, 22 April 1912

33 Noël Rothes, *New York Herald*, Paris edition, 22 April 1912, https://gallica.bnf.fr/ark:/12148/bpt6k41314276/f1.image with thanks to Philip Hind for this link

34 From Alfred Crawford's evidence to the American Inquiry, 1912, *Titanic Inquiry Project*, www.titanicinquiry.org/USInq/AmInq01Crawford01.php, and from Alfred Crawford's evidence to the British Inquiry, 1912, *Titanic Inquiry Project*, www.titanicinquiry.org/BOTInq/BOTInq16Crawford01.php

35 Ibid. American and British inquiries

36 Doree Flodin Soderman (granddaughter of Emma Bucknell), *Titanic Survivor: Emma Eliza Bucknell*, Gundi Publishing, 2008, https://store.titanichistoricalsociety.org/product/titanic-survivor-emma-eliza-bucknell

37 George Behe, '*Titanic*: The Long Night', unpublished manuscript, 2025, citing Emma Bucknell, *Philadelphia Inquirer*, 20 April 1912

38 Marie Grice Young, in George Behe, *On Board RMS Titanic: Memories of the Maiden Voyage*, The History Press, 2017, p.135

39 From Alfred Crawford's evidence to the American Inquiry, 1912, *Titanic Inquiry Project*, www.titanicinquiry.org/USInq/AmInq09Crawford01.php

40 Bruce Ismay, to the American Inquiry, 1912, *Titanic Inquiry Project*, www.titanicinquiry.org/USInq/AmInq01Rostron04.php

41 George Behe, *On Board RMS Titanic: Memories of the Maiden Voyage*, The History Press, 2017, pp.164, 364

42 Marie Grice Young, in George Behe, *On Board RMS Titanic: Memories of the Maiden Voyage*, The History Press, 2017, p.135

43 Anton Gill, *Titanic: The Real Story of the Construction of the World's Most Famous Ship*, Channel 4 Books, 2012, pp.164–5

44 From Thomas Jones' evidence to the American Inquiry, 1912, *Titanic Inquiry Project*, www.titanicinquiry.org/USInq/AmInq07Jones01.php

45 Noël Rothes, 1980-typed copy of her sworn statement to the American Inquiry, made to the British Vice-Consul at Altadena, California, in May 1912

46 Noël Rothes, letter to her parents, Thomas and Clementina Dyer-Edwardes, written on board *Carpathia*, 18 April 1912. (Original lost. This text taken from a typed copy of the original, made in 1980 by Eve Mackworth-Young.) Courtesy of the Leslie family

Six: Rescue

1 Noël Rothes, letter to her parents, Thomas and Clementina Dyer-Edwardes, written on board *Carpathia*, 18 April 1912. (Original lost. This text taken from a typed copy of the original, made in 1980 by Eve Mackworth-Young.) Courtesy of the Leslie family
2 Lawrence Beesley, *The Loss of the Titanic*, Houghton Mifflin, 1912, www.gutenberg.org/cache/epub/6675/pg6675-images.html
3 Ibid.
4 Tim Maltin, 'The hidden cause of the *Titanic* disaster', 5 January 2021, https://timmaltin.com/2021/01/05/thermal-inversion-titanic-disaster, also Tim Maltin, *Titanic: A Very Deceiving Night*, Malt House Publishing, 2012
5 Noël Rothes, letter to her parents, Thomas and Clementina Dyer-Edwardes, written on board *Carpathia*, 18 April 1912. (Original lost. This text taken from a typed copy of the original, made in 1980 by Eve Mackworth-Young.) Courtesy of the Leslie family
6 Marie Grice Young, in George Behe, *On Board RMS Titanic: Memories of the Maiden Voyage*, The History Press, 2017, p.135
7 Noël Rothes, *New York Herald*, Paris edition, 22 April 1912, https://gallica.bnf.fr/ark:/12148/bpt6k41314276/f1.image, with thanks to Philip Hind for this link
8 Fifth Office Lowe's Lifeboat Number 14, *Encyclopedia Titanica*, www.encyclopedia-titanica.org/titanic-survivor/harold-godfrey-lowe.html
9 Noël Rothes, letter to her parents, Thomas and Clementina Dyer-Edwardes, written on board *Carpathia*, 18 April 1912. (Original lost. This text taken from a typed copy of the original, made in 1980 by Eve Mackworth-Young.) Courtesy of the Leslie family
10 Thomas Jones, interview with *The Daily Telegraph*, 22 April 1912
11 Some reports say five hours, but Lifeboat Number 8 was one of the furthest from *Carpathia* because they'd spent so many hours rowing north in the opposite direction, towards 'the light'
12 Lawrence Beesley, *The Loss of the Titanic*, Houghton Mifflin, 1912, www.gutenberg.org/cache/epub/6675/pg6675-images.html
13 Noël Rothes, letter to her parents, Thomas and Clementina Dyer-Edwardes, written on board *Carpathia*, 18 April 1912. (Original lost. This text taken from a typed copy of the original, made in 1980 by Eve Mackworth-Young.) Courtesy of the Leslie family
14 Noël Rothes, interview, *Los Angeles Examiner*, 16 May 1912, https://libraryca.libanswers.com/loaderTicket?fid=4953037&type=0&key=0069c59eaf449530d9c46d6c39289348. With thanks to the California State Library for this link
15 George Behe, *On Board RMS Titanic: Memories of the Maiden Voyage*, The History Press, 2017, p.134, citing: Marie Grice Young, *Washington Post*, 21 April 1912
16 Arthur Rostron, *Home from the Sea*, Cassell & Co., 1931
17 From Thomas Jones' evidence to the American Inquiry, 1912, *Titanic Inquiry Project*, www.titanicinquiry.org/USInq/AmInq07Jones01.php
18 Captain Rostron, to the British Inquiry, 1912, *Titanic Inquiry Project*, www.titanicinquiry.org/BOTInq/BOTInq28Rostron02.php
19 Noël Rothes, letter to her parents, Thomas and Clementina Dyer-Edwardes, written on board *Carpathia*, 18 April 1912. (Original lost. This text taken from a typed copy of the original, made in 1980 by Eve Mackworth-Young.) Courtesy of the Leslie family
20 Harold Bride, Assistant Marconi Officer, to the American Inquiry, *Titanic Inquiry Project*, www.titanicinquiry.org/USInq/AmInq02Bride05.php
21 Ibid.
22 George Behe, https://wormstedt.com/GeorgeBehe/Page13.htm

Seven: On Board *Carpathia*

1 Noël Rothes, letter to her parents, Thomas and Clementina Dyer-Edwardes, written on board *Carpathia*, 18 April 1912. (Original lost. This text taken from a typed copy of the original, made in 1980 by Eve Mackworth-Young.) Courtesy of the Leslie family
2 Harold Cottam, evidence to the British Inquiry, 1912, *Titanic Inquiry Project*, www.titanicinquiry.org/BOTInq/BOTInq15Cottam01.php
3 Dr Rudi Newman
4 https://en.wikipedia.org/wiki/John_Simon,_1st_Viscount_Simon and D.J. Dutton, *Oxford Dictionary of National Biography*, 2004, www.oxforddnb.com/search?q=Simon%2C+John+Allsebrook%2C+first+Viscount+Simon+%281873%E2%80%931954%29
5 Harold Cottam, evidence to the British Inquiry, 1912, *Titanic Inquiry Project*, www.titanicinquiry.org/BOTInq/BOTInq15Cottam01.php and times from: Dr Rudi Newman
6 Noël Rothes, letter to her parents, Thomas and Clementina Dyer-Edwardes, written on board *Carpathia*, 18 April 1912. (Original lost. This text taken from a typed copy of the original, made in 1980 by Eve Mackworth-Young.) Courtesy of the Leslie family
7 Captain Arthur Rostron, evidence to the American Inquiry, 1912, *Titanic Inquiry Project*, www.titanicinquiry.org/USInq/AmInq01Rostron03.php
8 Guglielmo Marconi, evidence to the American Inquiry, 1912, *Titanic Inquiry Project*, www.titanicinquiry.org/USInq/AmInq01Marconi02.php
9 John Protasio, 'A *Titanic* Centennial', *Naval History*, Vol. 26, No. 2, April 2012, www.usni.org/magazines/naval-history-magazine/2012/april/titanic-centennial
10 Arthur Rostron, evidence to the American Inquiry, 1912, *Titanic Inquiry Project*, www.titanicinquiry.org/usinq/aminq01rostron01.php
11 Arthur Rostron, evidence to the American Inquiry, 1912, *Titanic Inquiry Project*, www.titanicinquiry.org/USInq/AmInq01Rostron02.php
12 Cyril Evans, evidence to the American Inquiry, 1912, *Titanic Inquiry Project*, www.titanicinquiry.org/USInq/AmInq08EvansCF01.php
13 Ibid.
14 American Inquiry, *Titanic Inquiry Project*, www.titanicinquiry.org/USInq/USReport/AmInqRep06.php
15 Noël Rothes, letter to her parents, Thomas and Clementina Dyer-Edwardes, written on board *Carpathia*, 18 April 1912. (Original lost. This text taken from a typed copy of the original, made in 1980 by Eve Mackworth-Young.) Courtesy of the Leslie family
16 Ibid.
17 Arthur Rostron, *Home from the Sea*, Cassell & Co., 1931
18 George Behe, *On Board RMS Titanic: Memories of the Maiden Voyage*, The History Press, 2017, p.366, citing: Elizabeth Shute, in Archibald Gracie, *The Truth About the Titanic*, Mitchell Kennerley, 1913, www.gutenberg.org/ebooks/67584
19 George Behe, Samuel Halpern et al., *Report into the Loss of the SS Titanic*, The History Press, 2016, pp.285–311
20 Gladys Cherry, letter to her mother, 18 April 1912, on board *Carpathia*; Hester Julian, *Memorials of Henry Forbes Julian* (Griffin, 1914); *Atlantic Daily Bulletin*; and George Behe, *On Board RMS Titanic: Memories of the Maiden Voyage*, The History Press, 2017, p.114
21 John Savile Judd was only 33 when he died, in 1912, www.wikitree.com/wiki/Judd-5879 and www.findagrave.com/memorial/263799930/john-savile-judd
22 *Fifeshire Advertiser*, 4 May 1912, p.3

Eight: Letters and Gifts

1 Gladys Cherry, Letter to Thomas Jones, May 1912, syndicated to newspapers, including *Wells Journal*, 30 May 1912, p.5; also in George Behe, *On Board RMS Titanic: Memories of the Maiden Voyage*, The History Press, 2017, p.200
2 *Titanic Connections*, www.titanicconnections.com/the-titanic/aftermath
3 Arthur Rostron, *Home from the Sea*, Cassell & Co., 1931
4 *Daily Echo*, 16 October 1999, www.dailyecho.co.uk/news/5632731.jeweller-fined-for-titanic-con, and BBC News, 20 November 1999, http://news.bbc.co.uk/1/hi/uk/529991.stm
5 Thomas Jones, Letter to Noël Rothes, 28 June 1912, reproduced with permission from Shelagh Oakes, Thomas Jones' granddaughter
6 Thomas Jones, Letter to Noël Rothes, 29 September 1912, reproduced with permission from Shelagh Oakes, Thomas Jones' granddaughter; also printed in Gareth Russell, *The Ship of Dreams*, William Collins, 2020, p.332
7 BBC News, 14 April 2012, www.bbc.co.uk/news/uk-england-17583924
8 Gladys Cherry, Letter to Thomas Jones, May 1912, syndicated to newspapers, including *Wells Journal*, 30 May 1912, p.5; also in George Behe, *On Board RMS Titanic: Memories of the Maiden Voyage*, The History Press, 2017, p.200
9 Ibid., *Wells Journal*
10 Fifth Officer Lowe, to the American Inquiry, 1912, *Titanic Inquiry Project*, www.titanicinquiry.org/USInq/AmInq05Lowe06.php, and from here: www.encyclopedia-titanica.org/titanic/lifeboats/lifeboat-14

Nine: What Went Wrong and What Changed Afterwards

1 Bruce Ismay, Chairman of the White Star Line, quoted in George Behe, 'How the *Titanic* Became "Unsinkable"', https://wormstedt.com/GeorgeBehe/page2.htm?fbclid=Iw
2 British Inquiry Report, 1912, *Titanic Inquiry Project*, www.titanicinquiry.org/BOTInq/BOTReport/BOTRepBoats.php
3 Ibid.
4 Bill Wormstedt et al., '*Titanic*: Which People were in What Lifeboat, A New Study', 2025, https://wormstedt.com/Lifeboat_Project/Lifeboat_Project_Survivors.html
5 British Inquiry Report, 1912, *Titanic Inquiry Project*, www.titanicinquiry.org/BOTInq/BOTReport/BOTRepBoats.php
6 Janet Dempsey, *Women and Children First*, at 25.21 minutes into her talk, https://media.nationalarchives.gov.uk/index.php/women-and-children-first, with thanks to Dr Rudi Newman for this reference
7 Mark Chirnside and Tim Maltin interviewed on *Titanic, Ship of Dreams*, 2025 podcast, Episode Eight, 'Every Man for Himself', www.noiser.com/titanic-ship-of-dreams/8-every-man-for-himself
8 George Behe, Samuel Halpern et al., *Report into the Loss of the SS Titanic*, The History Press, 2016, pp.212–13
9 *Titanic and Co.*, www.titanicandco.com/olympic/olympiccareer.html#involvement
10 George Behe, Samuel Halpern et al., *Report into the Loss of the SS Titanic*, The History Press, 2016, p.169

11 Ibid., pp.67–9
12 Ibid., pp.285–336, Lester J. Mitcham
13 American Inquiry Report, 1912, *Titanic Inquiry Project*, www.titanicinquiry.org/USInq/USReport/AmInqRepRaynor01.php
14 British Inquiry Report, 1912, *Titanic Inquiry Project*, www.titanicinquiry.org/BOTInq/BOTReport/botRepRec.php#a4
15 Amy Tikkanen, *Britannica* (online), updated 6 August 2025, www.britannica.com/topic/Titanic/Aftermath-and-investigation
16 British Inquiry conclusion, 1912, *Titanic Inquiry Project*, www.titanicinquiry.org/BOTInq/BOTReport/botRepAction.php
17 George Behe, Samuel Halpern et al., *Report into the Loss of the SS Titanic*, The History Press, 2016, p.240
18 International Radiotelegraph Convention ratified in Britain, https://treaties.fcdo.gov.uk/data/Library2/pdf/1913-TS0010.pdf
19 All SOLAS articles, regulations and text paraphrased by me, from George Behe, Samuel Halpern et al., *Report into the Loss of the SS Titanic*, The History Press, 2016, pp.240–6
20 SS *Eastland* disaster, https://en.wikipedia.org/wiki/SS_Eastland, additional information: Dr Rudi Newman
21 Emil Taussig, in George Behe, *On Board RMS Titanic: Memories of the Maiden Voyage*, The History Press, 2017, p.24
22 Ibid.
23 Ryan v. the White Star Line, www.bbc.co.uk/news/uk-northern-ireland-17612629, with thanks to Dr Rudi Newman
24 Lloyd's, 'Lloyd's and the *Titanic*', https://www.lloyds.com/titanic
25 Dr Rudi Newman, *Travelling to Tragedy*, PiXZ Books, 2017, p.10
26 George Behe
27 Lloyd's, 'Lloyd's and the *Titanic*', https://www.lloyds.com/titanic
28 Gareth Russell, *The Ship of Dreams*, William Collins, 2020, p.369, note 28
29 Limitation of Liability Hearings, 1912, *Titanic Inquiry Project*, www.titanicinquiry.org/lol/claims/countessofrothes-claim3.php
30 'Five Ways to Compute the Relative Value of a UK Pound Amount, 1270 to Present', *MeasuringWorth*, 2025, www.measuringworth.com/ukcompare/ and with thanks to Hugo Sells for pointing out that purchasing power comparisons vary depending upon whether a commodity, a wage, wealth or a project is being compared across years
31 Limitation of Liability Hearings, Final Decree, 1916, *Titanic Inquiry Project*, www.titanicinquiry.org/lol/finaldecree.php
32 Library of Congress, Blogs, '110 Years Later: *Titanic* Lawsuits Follow Tragedy', https://blogs.loc.gov/law/2022/04/110-years-later-titanic-lawsuits-follow-tragedy
33 Hale Law Firm, www.halelawfirm.com/blog/how-did-damage-caps-impact-titanic-survivor-lawsuits
34 Dr Rudi Newman, 'Lost in the Wreck of the Packet "*Titanic*"… The aftermath of the sinking from the perspective of Royal Mail', *Atlantic Daily Bulletin*, December 2015, pp.22–32
35 Limitation of Liability Hearings, Final Decree, 1912, *Titanic Inquiry Project*, www.titanicinquiry.org/lol/finaldecree.php
36 American National Archives and Records Administration (NARA), www.archives.gov/publications/prologue/2012/spring/titanic.html

37 Christopher Ward, *And the Band Played On*, Hodder & Stoughton, 2012, p.117
38 Eugene Nesmeyanov, 'How was the wreck of the *Titanic* discovered?', The History Press, 31 August 2018, https://thehistorypress.co.uk/article/how-was-the-wreck-of-the-titanic-discovered
39 https://en.wikipedia.org/wiki/Wreck_of_the_Titanic and Eugene Nesmeyanov, *The Titanic Expeditions*, The History Press, 2018, p.48
40 *Titanic: A Digital Resurrection*, Atlantic Studios, https://atlanticstudios.co.uk/work/titanic-the-digital-resurrection/
41 Unesco Protection for *Titanic*, www.bbc.co.uk/news/world-17629389, additional information: Dr Rudi Newman
42 Gov.uk, www.gov.uk/government/news/rms-titanic-wreck-to-be-protected-under-historic-treaty-with-us
43 Bruce Ismay, Chairman of the White Star Line, quoted in George Behe, 'How the *Titanic* Became "Unsinkable"', https://wormstedt.com/GeorgeBehe/page2.htm?fbclid=Iw

Ten: The Aftermath

1 Noël Rothes, *New York Herald*, Paris edition, 22 April 1912, https://gallica.bnf.fr/ark:/12148/bpt6k41314276/f1.image, with thanks to Philip Hind, Founder & Editor, *Encyclopedia Titanica* for this link
2 Noël Rothes, interview, *Los Angeles Examiner*, 16 May 1912, https://libraryca.libanswers.com/loaderTicket?fid=4953037&type=0&key=0069c59eaf449530d9c46d6c39289348. With thanks to the California State Library for this link
3 Dr Rudi Newman
4 Hester Julian, *Memorials of Henry Forbes Julian* (Griffin, 1914); *Atlantic Daily Bulletin*; and George Behe, Samuel Halpern et al., *On Board RMS Titanic: Memories of the Maiden Voyage*, The History Press, 2017, pp.97–9
5 Noël Rothes, Letter to May Goodman, her cousin, from the Plaza Hotel, New York, 26 April 1912. Courtesy of the Leslie family
6 '*Titanic* Survivors Tell Tales of Awful Horror', *The Valentine Democrat*, 25 April 1912, p.7, Nebraska Newspapers, https://nebnewspapers.unl.edu/lccn/sn95069780/1912-04-25/ed-1/seq-7/#words=SURVIVORS+survivors+TITANIC+Titanic, also here, but with no newspaper name or date, https://nebnewspapers.unl.edu/lccn/sn95069780/1912-04-25/ed-1/seq-7.pdf
7 Lawrence Beesley, *The Loss of the Titanic*, Houghton Mifflin, 1912, www.gutenberg.org/cache/epub/6675/pg6675-images.html
8 Andrew Wilson, *Shadow of the Titanic*, Simon & Schuster, 2012, p.9
9 Ibid.
10 Noël Rothes, *New York Herald*, Paris edition, 22 April 1912, https://gallica.bnf.fr/ark:/12148/bpt6k41314276/f1.image with thanks to Philip Hind for this link
11 Tim Cornwell, 'The Scots engineers who fought to the last to save the *Titanic*', *The Scotsman*, 11 April 2012, www.scotsman.com/news/the-scots-engineers-who-fought-to-the-last-to-save-the-titanic-1634388; Gordon Masterton, www.ice.org.uk/what-is-civil-engineering/meet-the-engineers/gordon-masterton-ices-141st-president
12 Dr Rudi Newman, *Travelling to Tragedy*, PiXZ Books, 2017, p.22

13 Gladys Cherry, third letter to her mother, from New York, 19 April 1912; Hester Julian, *Memorials of Henry Forbes Julian* (Griffin, 1914); *Atlantic Daily Bulletin*; and George Behe, *On Board RMS Titanic: Memories of the Maiden Voyage*, The History Press, 2017, pp.199–200

14 Ibid.

15 Norman Evelyn Rothes, Letter to Thomas Dyer-Edwardes, from New York, 7 May 1912, courtesy of the Leslie family

16 Noël Rothes, Letter to May Goodman, from the Plaza Hotel, New York, 26 April 1912, courtesy of the Leslie family

17 Bruce Ismay, to the American Inquiry, *Titanic Inquiry Project*, www.titanicinquiry.org/USInq/AmInq01Ismay01.php

18 British Titanic Society, https://britishtitanicsociety.com/home-at-last

19 Thomas Jones' postcard to his wife-to-be Clara Moulton, from New York, before he knew he would be subpoenaed by the American Inquiry. Undated, from Eric Torr, of the Cemaes Bay History Group and J. Richard Williams. Reproduced courtesy of Shelagh Oakes, granddaughter

20 Lists of *Titanic* crew (and passengers) who gave evidence to the American Inquiry, *Titanic Inquiry Project*, www.titanicinquiry.org/USInq/AmInq01Indxa.php (A-H) and www.titanicinquiry.org/USInq/AmInq01Indx2a.php (I-Z)

21 *The New York Times*, 20 April 1912, www.nytimes.com/1912/04/20/archives/titanics-seamen-at-prayer-service-all-deeply-moved-many-weeping.html and information about piers and memorials, https://abisaab.wordpress.com/2012/05/16/the-titanic-and-new-york

22 *Titanic* Inquiry moved to Washington, www.senate.gov/about/powers-procedures/investigations/titanic.htm

23 With thanks to Dr Rudi Newman

24 Noël Rothes, interview, *Los Angeles Examiner*, 16 May 1912,https://libraryca.libanswers.com/loaderTicket?fid=4953037&type=0&key=0069c59eaf449530d9c46d6c39289348. With thanks to the California State Library for this link

25 Thomas Jones, interview with a friend, https://x.com/Liverpool1207/status/1804171712453370044/photo/4

26 Noël Rothes' letter, 7 August 1955, to Walter Lord, for his book, *A Night to Remember*, LMQ/7/2/20 Caird Library, National Maritime Museum, Greenwich, p.9, reverse

27 LMQ/7 Caird Library, National Maritime Museum Archive, Greenwich, www.rmg.co.uk/collections/objects/rmgc-object-483723

28 Interviewed by Senator Smith on Day 1 of the Inquiry, 19 April 1912, *Titanic Inquiry Project*, www.titanicinquiry.org/USInq/AmInq01Crawford01.php and interviewed by Mr Butler Aspinall on Day 16 of the Inquiry, 4 June 1912, *Titanic Inquiry Project*, www.titanicinquiry.org/BOTInq/BOTInq16Crawford01.php

29 From Thomas Jones' evidence to the American Inquiry, 1912, *Titanic Inquiry Project*, www.titanicinquiry.org/USInq/AmInq07Jones01.php

30 Interviewed by Senator Smith on Day 12 of the Inquiry, 2 May 1912, *Titanic Inquiry Project*, www.titanicinquiry.org/USInq/AmInq12White01.php

31 Dr Rudi Newman, *Travelling to Tragedy*, PiXZ Books, 2017, p.41

Postscript: The *Lady Rothes*

1 Thomas Dyer-Edwardes quoted in *The Fraserburgh Herald and Northern Counties Advertiser*, 10 August 1915

2 Randy Bryan Bigham, 'A Matter of Course', *Encyclopedia Titanica*, www.encyclopedia-titanica.org/countess.html

3 RNLI Facebook page, www.facebook.com/RNLIFraserburgh/posts/titanic-survivor-lady-rothes-15th-april-1912the-titanic-the-worlds-biggest-ever-/835326348639606

Biographies of Noël Rothes and Thomas Jones

1 Randy Bryan Bigham, 'A Matter of Course', *Encyclopedia Titanica*, www.encyclopedia-titanica.org/countess.html

2 *Dundee Courier*, 12 August 1914, p.2, with thanks to James Leslie (no relation) for this information; *History of Highland Hospitals*, www.historyofhighlandhospitals.com

3 Scottish Red Cross Detachments, 1914–1918, Scottish Voluntary Aid Detachment Numbers and Locations, Medical Services (Home and Abroad), *The Great War (1914–1918) Forum*, www.greatwarforum.org/topic/241447-scottish-voluntary-aid-detachment-numbers-and-locations

4 Description of an Aunt Sally stall, www.traditionalsports.org/traditional-sports/europe/aunt-sally-england.html

5 With thanks to Graeme McDonald, Military Historian, for this information

6 Olive Schreiner, d.1920. Words from Ralph Iron (pseudonym), *The Story of an African Farm*, Chapman and Hall, 1883, www.gutenberg.org/files/1441/1441-h/1441-h.htm

7 https://titanic.fandom.com/wiki/Thomas_William_Jones

8 *CLIP, Crew List Index Project*, Friends, 1886, www.crewlist.org.uk/people/transcript?DocumentId=112360

9 From Thomas Jones' evidence to the American Inquiry, 1912, *Titanic Inquiry Project*, www.titanicinquiry.org/USInq/AmInq07Jones01.php

10 With thanks to the Southampton Archives, Richard Arthur, for this.

11 *Oceanic* foundered off Foula, https://passengers.history.sa.gov.au/node/1005320

12 The BAR Lightship, www.old-merseytimes.co.uk/lightships.html

13 uboat.net, https://uboat.net/allies/merchants/crews/ship571.html

14 Plaque in Thomas Jones' memory, at 84 Jacob Street, Liverpool, in 2021, https://commons.wikimedia.org/wiki/File:Jones_plaque_at_84_Jacob_Street,_Liverpool.jpg, www.youtube.com/watch?v=UpaGdxZy3eU and www.dailypost.co.uk/news/nostalgia/overruled-anglesey-hero-wasnt-allowed-21653819

Bibliography

Articles, Books, Letters & Newspapers

Dr Nick Barratt, *Lost Voices from the Titanic*, Preface Publishing, 2009

BBC interview with Nell Jones and Angela Young, www.bbc.co.uk/news/uk-england-17583924

BBC News, 20 November 1999, http://news.bbc.co.uk/1/hi/uk/529991.stm

BBC News, 14 April 2012, www.bbc.co.uk/news/uk-england-17583924

BBC News NI, 18 April 2012, www.bbc.co.uk/news/uk-northern-ireland-17612629

Lawrence Beesley, *The Loss of the Titanic: Its Story and Its Lessons*, Houghton Mifflin, 1912, www.gutenberg.org/files/6675/6675-h/6675-h.htm. Reprinted as: *I Survived the Titanic*, with a foreword by Beesley's grandson, Nicholas Wade, Amberley Publishing, 2011

George Behe, 'The Fate of Jack Phillips', https://wormstedt.com/GeorgeBehe/Page13.htm

George Behe, 'How the *Titanic* Became "Unsinkable"', https://wormstedt.com/GeorgeBehe/page2.htm?fbclid=Iw

George Behe, *On Board RMS Titanic: Memories of the Maiden Voyage*, The History Press, 2017

George Behe, Samuel Halpern et al., *Report into the Loss of the SS Titanic*, The History Press, 2016

George Behe, '*Titanic*: The Long Night', unpublished manuscript, 2025

Randy Bigham, 'A Matter of Course', *Encyclopedia Titanica*, www.encyclopedia-titanica.org/countess.html

Blue Hill Observatory & Science Center Handbook, Milton, MA, www.bluehill.org/handbook/Tables/Knots_to_MPH_Conversion.pdf

Victoria Brown, *The Death Ship: Recovering the Bodies of Titanic's Dead*, The History Press, 2025

Carolinian Newspaper, 26 August 2024, https://caro.news/laroche-the-only-black-man-on-the-titanic

Daily Echo, 16 October 1999, www.dailyecho.co.uk/news/5632731.jeweller-fined-for-titanic-con

Kellie Carter Jackson, *Untold Stories of the Titanic: The Only Black Passenger*, Noble Maritime Collection, 2022, www.youtube.com/watch?v=dzf1SVLAE74

Sewell Chan, *The New York Times*, 6 November 2009, https://archive.nytimes.com/cityroom.blogs.nytimes.com/2009/11/06/remembering-jack-binns-heroic-radio-operator

Mark Chirnside, *Mark Chirnside's Reception Room*, https://markchirnside.co.uk/articles, specifically: 'Big Ships and Small Boats'; '*Titanic*'s Lifeboats: Fact & Fiction'; '*Titanic*'s Lifeboats: An Increased Capacity'; and 'FAQ: Which Was *Olympic*'s Fastest Crossing?'

The Daily Graphic, 30 April 1912

The Daily Telegraph, 20 April 1912 & 22 April 1912

Richard Davenport-Hines, *Titanic Lives: Migrants and Millionaires, Conmen and Crew*, HarperPress, 2012

Janet Dempsey, *Women and Children First*, The National Archives, https://media.nationalarchives.gov.uk/index.php/women-and-children-first

Dundee Courier, 12 August 1914

Leila Salloum Elias, 'Alien Passengers: Syrians Aboard the *Titanic*', www.palestine-studies.org/sites/default/files/jq-articles/JQ-52-Salloum-Alien_Passengers_2_0.pdf

Encyclopedia Titanica, Thomas William Jones biography, www.encyclopedia-titanica.org/titanic-survivor/thomas-william-jones.html

Fifeshire Advertiser, 4 May 1912

'Five Ways to Compute the Relative Value of a UK Pound Amount, 1270 to Present', *MeasuringWorth*, 2025, www.measuringworth.com/ukcompare

Fraserburgh Herald and Northern Counties Advertiser, 10 August 1915 & 27 March 1998

Anton Gill, *Titanic: The Real Story of the Construction of the World's Most Famous Ship*, Channel 4 Books, 2012

Hale Law Firm, 'How did Damage Caps impact *Titanic* Survivor lawsuits?', www.halelawfirm.com/blog/how-did-damage-caps-impact-titanic-survivor-lawsuits

Hester Julian, *Memorials of Henry Forbes Julian*, Griffin, 1914

Letters of Gladys Cherry, Thomas Jones, Noël Rothes and Evelyn Rothes (all attributions in the Notes)

Library of Congress, Blogs, '110 Years Later: *Titanic* Lawsuits Follow Tragedy', https://blogs.loc.gov/law/2022/04/110-years-later-titanic-lawsuits-follow-tragedy

Liverpool Echo, 15 March 1956

Lloyd's, 'Lloyd's and the *Titanic*', https://www.lloyds.com/titanic

Walter Lord, *A Night to Remember*, R.V. Holt, 1955

Los Angeles Examiner, 16 May 1912

Paul Louden-Brown, *Titanic Belfast*, www.titanicbelfast.com/history-of-titanic/titanic-stories/titanic-food-for-all-classes

Tim Maltin, 'The *Frankfurt* and the *Titanic*', 10 April 2019, https://timmaltin.com/2019/04/10/frankfurt-titanic

Tim Maltin, 'The hidden cause of the *Titanic* disaster', 5 January 2021, https://timmaltin.com/2021/01/05/thermal-inversion-titanic-disaster

Tim Maltin, *Titanic: A Very Deceiving Night*, Malt House Publishing, 2012

Lester J. Mitcham, 1999–2001, www.encyclopedia-titanica.org/titanic-statistics.html

Eugene Nesmeyanov, 'How was the wreck of the *Titanic* discovered?', 31 August 2018, https://thehistorypress.co.uk/article/how-was-the-wreck-of-the-titanic-discovered

Eugene Nesmeyanov, *The Titanic Expeditions*, The History Press, 2018

New York Herald, Paris edition, 11 April 1912, https://gallica.bnf.fr/ark:/12148/bpt6k4131416d/f1.image

New York Herald, New York and Paris editions, 21 April 1912, https://gallica.bnf.fr/ark:/12148/bpt6k4131426s/f1.image

New York Herald, New York and Paris editions, 22 April 1912, www.encyclopedia-titanica.org/titanic-the-countess-of-rothes-and-the-phantom-light.html, https://gallica.bnf.fr/ark:/12148/bpt6k4131416d/f1.image

New York Post, 18 May 2023, https://nypost.com/2023/05/18/insane-image-reveals-titanic-compared-to-modern-day-cruise-ship

New York Times, 20 April 1912, www.nytimes.com/1912/04/20/archives/titanics-seamen-at-prayer-service-all-deeply-moved-many-weeping.html

Dr Rudi Newman, 'Another Rivetting Article … – an Historical Rejoinder to Metallurgical Studies of the *Titanic* Disaster', *Atlantic Daily Bulletin*, September 2012, pp. 18–30, www.academia.edu/2441774/Another_Rivetting_Article_an_Historical_Rejoinder_to_Metallurgical_Studies_of_the_Titanic_Disaster

Dr Rudi Newman, 'Lost in the Wreck of the Packet "*Titanic*"… The aftermath of the sinking from the perspective of Royal Mail', *Atlantic Daily Bulletin*, December 2015

Dr Rudi Newman, '*Titanic*'s Boilers – A New Theory', *Atlantic Daily Bulletin*, September 2014, pp. 13–15, www.academia.edu/25269010/Titanics_Boilers_A_New_Theory

Dr Rudi Newman, *Travelling to Tragedy*, PiXZ Books, 2017

Samantha Pak, 'The Six Chinese Men who Survived *Titanic*', https://joysauce.com/442-the-six-chinese-men-who-survived-the-titanic

John Protasio, 'A *Titanic* Centennial', *Naval History*, Vol. 26, No. 2, April 2012, www.usni.org/magazines/naval-history-magazine/2012/april/titanic-centennial

Antoine Resche, 'European Migrants' Crossings to the United States (1880–1925)', *Encyclopédie d'histoire numérique de l'Europe* (online), 2 July 2024, https://ehne.fr/en/node/14184

Arthur Rostron, *Home from the Sea*, Macmillan, 1931

Gareth Russell, *The Ship of Dreams*, William Collins, 2020

Ryan v. the White Star Line, www.bbc.co.uk/news/uk-northern-ireland-17612629

Olive Schreiner, *The Story of an African Farm*, Chapman and Hall, 1883, published under the pseudonym Ralph Iron

Shipbuilder, 1910 & 1911

Amy Tikkanen, *Britannica*, updated 6 August 2025, www.britannica.com/topic/Titanic/Aftermath-and-investigation

Valentine Democrat, 25 April 1912, Nebraska Newspapers

Christopher Ward, *And the Band Played On*, Hodder & Stoughton, 2012

John Welshman, *Titanic: The Last Night of a Small Town*, Oxford University Press, 2012

Andrew Wilson, *Shadow of the Titanic*, Simon & Schuster, 2012

Bill Wormstedt, Tad Fitch and George Behe, with contributions by Sam Halpern and J. Kent Layton, '[Lifeboat] Launch Times Re-Examined', https://wormstedt.com/Titanic/lifeboats/lifeboattable2.htm, with supporting information here: '*Titanic*: The Lifeboat Launching Sequence Re-Examined', https://wormstedt.com/Titanic/lifeboats/lifeboats.htm

Bill Wormstedt et al., '*Titanic*: Which People Were in What Lifeboat, A New Study', 2025, https://wormstedt.com/Lifeboat_Project/Lifeboat_Project_Survivors.html

Websites

American National Archives and Records Administration (NARA), www.archives.gov/publications/prologue/2012/spring/titanic.html

CLIP, Crew List Index Project, https://www.crewlist.org.uk

Encyclopedia Titanica, www.encyclopedia-titanica.org
Everybody's Cyclopedia v.5, https://catalog.hathitrust.org/Record/007647400
German U-boats of both World Wars, https://uboat.net
History on the Net, www.historyonthenet.com
Oxford Dictionary of National Biography, www.oxforddnb.com
Scottish Red Cross Detachments, 1914–1918, Scottish Voluntary Aid Detachment Numbers and Locations, Medical Services (Home and Abroad), *The Great War (1914–1918) Forum*, www.greatwarforum.org/topic/241447-scottish-voluntary-aid-detachment-numbers-and-locations
Titanic and Co., www.titanicandco.com/olympic/olympiccareer.html#involvement
Titanic Connections, www.titanicconnections.com/the-titanic/aftermath
Titanic Historical Society, https://titanichistoricalsociety.org
The Titanic Inquiry Project, www.titanicinquiry.org/about.php

Podcasts

The Rest is History, *The Titanic* series, 2024, https://www.youtube.com/playlist?list=PLEbAHi3fZpuHWj1LjhVQiQ8FER453PX8N
Titanic: Ship of Dreams, Noiser Productions, 2025, www.bbc.co.uk/programmes/p0j1vz3z

Films

Titanic: A Digital Resurrection, Atlantic Studios, https://atlanticstudios.co.uk/work/titanic-the-digital-resurrection
Titanic: Building the World's Largest Ship, Channel 4, April 2022, www.channel4.com/programmes/titanic-building-the-worlds-largest-ship
Titanic Sinks Tonight, BBC, www.bbc.co.uk/programmes/m002hyvg

If you'd like to book my illustrated talk about *The Aristocrat and the Able Seaman* for your history or literary society, WI, club, conference or any gathering interested in *Titanic*, you can, at my website: www.angela-young.co.uk/talks.

Index

Page references in *italic* text indicate an illustration

About the Author

© Adrian Pope

ANGELA YOUNG is a writer with two novels under her belt: *The Dance of Love* and *Speaking of Love*. Long inspired by her great-grandmother's *Titanic* papers, she developed a talk to present her story and the story of the able seaman in whose lifeboat her great-grandmother, Noël Rothes, survived. Through those papers, Young reveals the stark truth behind the tragedy. She writes a monthly blog that often includes *Titanic*-related topics. She has also previously written about *Titanic* for *YOU* magazine.